THE AIRCRAFT

TYPE: Two-seat general-purpose jet trainer.

WINGS: Cantilever mid-wing monoplane. Wing section NACA 64A212 (modified). Thickness/chord ratio 12%. All-metal two-spar structure. Interchangeable all-metal ailerons, with hydraulic boost. Large all-metal trailing-edge flaps.

FUSELAGE: All-metal semi-monocoque structure in three main sections: forward fuselage containing equipment bay and cockpit; centre fuselage housing power plant, fuel and wing carry-through structure; and rear fuselage, carrying the arrester hook and a hydraulically-actuated airbrake on each side of the fuselage.

TAIL UNIT: Cantilever all-metal structure. Each half of tailplane and elevators interchangeable. Elevators boosted hydraulically. Rudder manually controlled. Trim tabs in elevators and rudder.

LANDING GEAR: Retractable tricycle type. Oleopneumatic shock-absorbers. Hydraulic retraction. Main units retract inward into wings. Nosewheel retracts forward into fuselage. Goodyear aircooled single-disc hydraulic brakes. Retractable arrester hook.

North American Columbus Divis T-2 Buckeye Production

Charge No.	Type	Quantity	USN Se
NA-249	T2J-1 (T-2A)	6	144217-14
NA-253	T2J-1 (T-2A)	121	145996-146015
			147430-147530
NA-266	T2J-1 (T-2A)	90	148150-148239
NA-280	YT-2B	1	145997
NA-288	T-2B	10	152382-152391
NA-291	T-2B	36	152440-152475
NA-294	T-2B	18	153538-153555
NA-310	T-2B	33	155206-155238
	YT-2C	1	152382
NA-310	T-2C	3	155239-155241
NA-318	T-2C	48	156686-156733
NA-332	T-2C	36	157030-157065
NA-340	T-2C	24	158310-158333
NA-346	T-2C	36	158575-158610
NA-352	T-2C	36	158876-158911
NA-367	T-2C	24	159150-159173
NA-380	T-2C	24	159704-159727

Venezuela

NA-358	T-2D	12	159330-159341
NA-398	T-2D	12	160228-160239

Note: Venezuela assigns its own serial numbers.

Greece

NA-396	T-2E	40	160059-160093

ISBN: 978-0-942612-15-8

© 1987

S. Ginter, 1754 Warfield Cir.,
Simi Valley, California 93063.

Steve Ginter

CONTRIBUTORS

Roger Besecker, Ben Burger, Lt. Greg Craigmiles USN, John Elliott (Naval Aviation History), Ted Goldstone, Joel Griggs, Gene Holmberg, Clay Jansson, Maurice Landi (Matchbox), William T. Larkins, Robert Lawson, CDR. Dick Lear USN, Dave Menard, Fred Roos, Larry Smalley, Bob Stollof, William Swisher, Dent Williams (Rockwell International), Nick Williams and Stan Wyckoff.

Rockwell (North American) T-2 Buckeye Specification

	T-2A	T-2B	T-2C/D
Power Plant			
Type	One J34-WE-48	Two J60-P-6	Two J85-GE-4
Take-off thrust, each, lb (kg)	3,400 (1 540)	3,000 (1 360)	2,950 (1 338)
Performance			
Max speed, mph (km/h)	488 (785)	521 (838)	521 (838)
at an altitude of ft (m)	25,000 (7 620)	25,000 (7 620)	25,000 (7 620)
Initial rate of climb, ft/min (m/sec)	5,000 (25,4)	6,560 (33,3)	6,200 (31,5)
Service ceiling, ft (m)	40,000 (12 192)	40,664 (12 394	40,414 (12 318)
Max range, mls (km)	964 (1 550)	908 (1 461)	908 (1 461)
Weights			
Empty, lb (kg)	8,006 (3 631)	7,630 (3 460)	8,115 (3 680)
max take-off, lb (kg)	11,498 (5 215)	13,180 (5 978)	13,180 (5 978)
Dimensions			
Span over tip tanks, ft, in (m)	38,2 (11,63)	38,2 (11,63)	38,2 (11,63)
Length, ft, in (m)	38,8 (11,79)	38,8 (11,79)	38,8 (11,79)
Height, ft, in (m)	14,9 (4,50)	15,0 (4,57)	15,0 (4,57)
Wing area, sq ft (m2)	255 (23,69)	255 (23,69)	255 (23,69)
U/c track, ft, in (m)	18,5 (5,62)	18,5 (5,62)	18,5 (5,62)

In 1956 the United States Navy issued the requirements for an all-purpose jet trainer to America's aviation industry. The requirements called for an aircraft capable of handling the total jet training syllabus from transition and intermediate jet training to carrier qualification, gunnery training and advanced training.

North American Aviation, the major producer of Navy training aircraft for many years with the SNJ and T-28 (see Naval Fighters #5 the North American T-28 Trojan), was chosen to build the new jet trainer, designated the T2J-1 "Buckeye". One aspect of the T2J's design which helped North American win the contract was the fact that proven components and equipment would be used wherever possible and therefore reduce lead time needed to test those components. The control system was essentially the same as found in the T-28C with an added hydraulic boost package, and the wings were derived from North American's first Jet, the FJ-1 Fury (see Naval Fighters #7, the North American FJ-1 Fury).

North American received an initial contract for six T2J-1 aircraft originally designated YT2J-1 (and assigned the North American designation NA-241) in early 1956. A second contract for 121 T2J-1s (NA-253) was made at the end of 1956, and a third for 90 T2J-1s (NA-266) was placed in February 1959.

The first YT2J-1 was rolled out at North American's Columbus, Ohio, plant on 27 December 1957 and made its first flight on 31 January 1958 with Richard Wenzell at the controls. Minor difficulties with the landing gear were experienced during this first flight, but were corrected immediately. By the third flight and its first public demonstration on 10 February 1958, the natural metal YT2J-1 was painted the standard international orange and white training aircraft scheme. Soon after this flight, the YT2J-1 was taken to Palmdale, Calif., for continued testing.

Navy pilots evaluated this aircraft at Palmdale and three additional YT2J-1s at the Naval Air Test Center, NAS Patuxent River, Maryland. After carrier suitability tests were conducted aboard the USS Antietam (CVS-36) in May 1959 the T2J-1 (T-2A in 1962) was cleared for introduction into the Training Command. The first T2J-1 was delivered to NAS Pensacola on 9 July 1959.

Since the T2J-1 did not have a name, a contest in the Training Command was conducted in February 1959, with the winning name "Buckeye" being announced on 3 June 1959. The name, of course, refers to the state in which the T2J-1 was built, Ohio, which is called the "Buckeye state".

The T-2A proved to be a capable and excellent basic jet training aircraft, with but one shortcoming: power. The T-2A was powered by a single Westinghouse J34-WE-48 engine of 3,400 lb. of thrust, an engine which was first developed for the Navy in 1944. This single, obsolete turbojet was chosen instead of the later more powerful dual engine system of the

T2J-1 146001 on a early test flight, note early da-glo orange and white color scheme. (MFR.)

T-2B and T-2C simply because it was the only available powerplant in 1956 capable of doing the job. By 1960 modern lightweight efficent small turbojets became available and the Navy awarded North American a 3.3 million dollar contract on 26 January 1962 to modify two T-2As to twin-engines. The engines used were two Pratt & Whitney J60-P-6s. The J60's combined thrust (6,000 Lbs.) was over 70% more than the single J34s and the reliability of two engines almost completely eliminated engine related accidents in the "Buckeye".

Since the T-2A was designed with ease of maintenance in mind the single J-34 was slung under the fuselage. This design feature made it relatively simple to modify the under-fuselage to carry the two new J60s. The engines were slung side-by-side and the air intakes were enlarged to accomadate the increased airflow requirements.

The YT-2B (145997) (NA-280) made its first flight on 30 August 1962, and after Navy evaluation was completed an initial order was placed for 10 T-2Bs (NA-288) on 3 March 1964. Total T-2B production eventually reached 97 aircraft, with the 34th, and subsequent T-2B having a 50 gal. fuel tank installed in each wing's leading edge. This increase in fuel enabled the T-2B to better and more safely conduct the carrier qualification phase of the student's training.

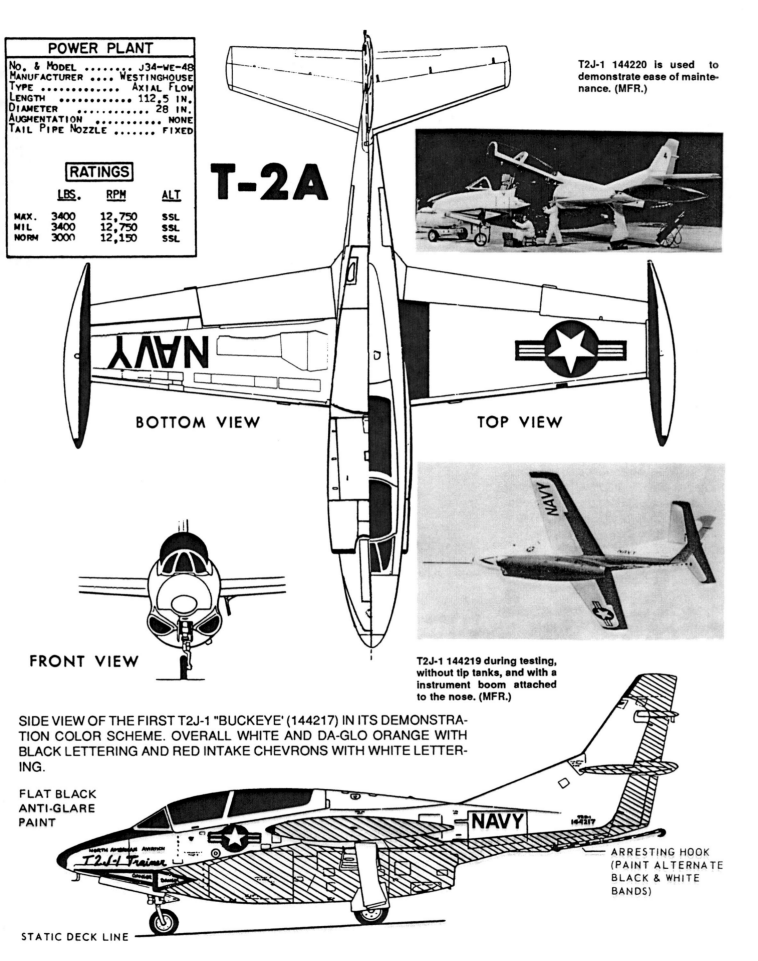

POWER PLANT

No. & Model J34-WE-48
Manufacturer .... Westinghouse
Type .... Axial Flow
Length .... 112.5 in.
Diameter .... 28 in.
Augmentation .... None
Tail Pipe Nozzle .... Fixed

RATINGS

	LBS.	RPM	ALT
MAX.	3400	12,750	SSL
MIL	3400	12,750	SSL
NORM	3000	12,150	SSL

T-2A

T2J-1 144220 is used to demonstrate ease of maintenance. (MFR.)

BOTTOM VIEW

TOP VIEW

FRONT VIEW

T2J-1 144219 during testing, without tip tanks, and with a instrument boom attached to the nose. (MFR.)

SIDE VIEW OF THE FIRST T2J-1 "BUCKEYE' (144217) IN ITS DEMONSTRA-TION COLOR SCHEME. OVERALL WHITE AND DA-GLO ORANGE WITH BLACK LETTERING AND RED INTAKE CHEVRONS WITH WHITE LETTER-ING.

FLAT BLACK
ANTI-GLARE
PAINT

NAVY

T2J-1
144217

ARRESTING HOOK
(PAINT ALTERNATE
BLACK & WHITE
BANDS)

STATIC DECK LINE

3

When compared to the T-2A, the T-2B's increased power provided the following improvements in performance: increased service ceiling to 42,000 ft., decreased take-off distance by 1805 feet, and increased range by 165 nautical miles. Having two engines and thereby two primary hydraulic systems, the T-2B had a higher safety factor that the T-2A. More modern avionics equipment was installed including the AN/APX-64 (V) identification system, which created a definite improvement during instrument conditions and cross-country flights. Despite the increased number and complexity of systems, the T-2B required only slightly more maintenance.

In 1967 the Navy placed a 2.2 million dollar contract to convert the first T-2B (152382) to the more cost effective General Electric J85-GE-4 turbojets. The combined thrust of the J85s was 5,900 lbs., which provided the new T-2C series with virtually the same performance as the T-2B.

First flight of the YT-2C (152382) took place on 17 April 1968 and the first production T-2C followed the last T-2B down the assembly line. Eventual production stopped at 231 T-2C aircraft.

T2J-1 148209 seen in factory fresh finish. Intake lip is black, and gear door edges are red as well as the ejection triangles and intake chevrons. (R.F. Besecker)

In flight view of T2J-1 in the early color scheme. (MFR.)

The YT-2B 145997, a converted T-2A, showing the redesigned under fuselage with twin engines and enlarged intakes. (MFR.)

YT-2B 145997 as it looked originally. Natural metal overall with black markings.

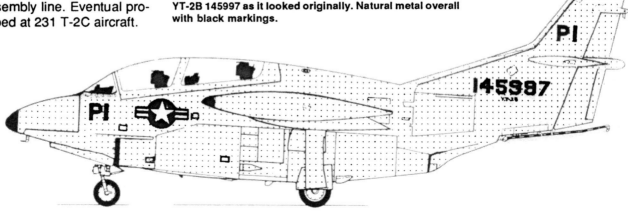

4

YT-2B 145997 after being designated T-2B and painted in standard training colors. (via Clay Jansson)

A Venezuelan T-2D from the first batch of 12, which were painted in the standard USN color scheme. Note belly antennae unique to Venezuela. National insignia and tail stripes are yellow-blue-red.

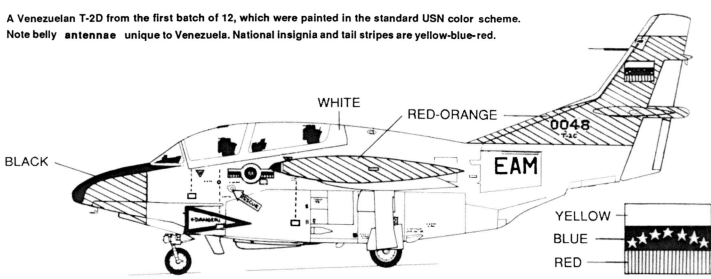

WHITE

RED-ORANGE

BLACK

0048
T-2C

EAM

YELLOW
BLUE
RED

Venezuelan T-2D from the second batch of 12, which was painted in the same tactical camouflage scheme as Hellenic T-2Es, seen below. These aircraft were ground attack machines.

WHITE STAR AND YELLOW WINGS ON TAIL

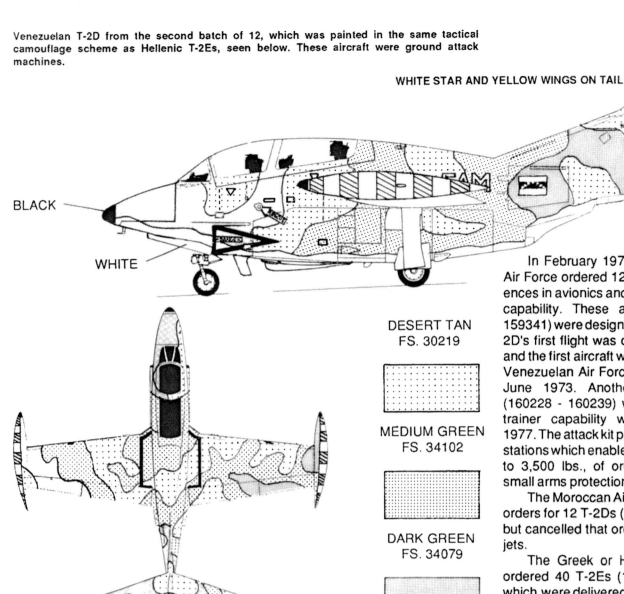

BLACK

WHITE

WHITE

RED-ORANGE

DESERT TAN
FS. 30219

MEDIUM GREEN
FS. 34102

DARK GREEN
FS. 34079

Greek or Hellenic Air Force T-2E 160059 in the desert tan and green olive drab tactical scheme. Landing gear and wheel wells are white, national insignia blue and white. (MFR.)

In February 1972 the Venezuelan Air Force ordered 12 T-2Cs with differences in avionics and no carrier landing capability. These aircraft (159330 - 159341) were designated T-2Ds. The T-2D's first flight was on 13 March 1973 and the first aircraft was delivered to the Venezuelan Air Force Academy on 20 June 1973. Another twelve T-2Ds (160228 - 160239) with a dual strike/trainer capability were delivered in 1977. The attack kit provides for six wing stations which enable the T-2 to carry up to 3,500 lbs., of ordnance, and with small arms protection for the fuel tanks.

The Moroccan Air Force had placed orders for 12 T-2Ds (160228 - 160239), but cancelled that order in favor of Alfa jets.

The Greek or Hellenic Air Force ordered 40 T-2Es (160059 - 160098) which were delivered in 1976 and 1977. The T-2E was generally similar to the T-2C, except for different electronics equipment and the incorporation of the attack kit as described above.

WEAPONS SYSTEMS
ARMAMENT SYSTEM

Practice stores and packages which can be installed at an external station on each wing include bombs, air-to-air and air-to-ground rockets, gun pods and aerial tow targets. An armament control system is provided for selecting and firing. The fire control system provides aiming and radar ranging.

EXTERNAL STORES
GUN PODS

The strafing and aerial gunnery configuration consists of a nonjettisonable .50-caliber gun pod, attached to an Aero 1A subcaliber adapter, at each wing store station. Each package contains an M2 gas-operated automatic gun with a self-contained pneumatic charger and capacity for 100 rounds of ammunition. The guns are controlled through switches on the center pedestal armament panel and fired by depressing the trigger switch on the forward cockpit stick grip. Safety provisions are incorporated within the armament control system to prevent inadvertent firing of the guns on the ground.

STORE PYLONS

An Aero 15D bomb rack is mounted in each wing store station pylon. A variety of ordnance may be carried on each rack or on an A/A37B-3 practice multiple bomb rack attached to the Aero 15D; however, all confrigurations carried must be symmetric. Bombs may be released from a single station or from both stations simultaneously, and can also be jettisoned through use of the jettison button. A single MK 15 Mod 4 (100-pound) or MK 86 (141-pound) practice bomb may be carried directly on each pylon. By installing an Aero 1A subcaliber adapter on each Aero 15 D rack, each pylon is made capable of carrying other stores.

PRACTICE MULTIPLE BOMB RACK

The A/A37B-3 PMBR is designed to carry from one to six practice bombs, which cannot normally be suspended directly on the store pylon racks. The following practice bombs can be carried with this installation.

MK 76 Mod 4, Mod 5, and Mod 6 (25-pound), six each
MK 106 Mod 2 and Mod 3 (5-pound), six each

TOW TARGET EQUIPMENT

When armament provisions are installed, sleeve- or banner-type aerial targets may be carried, launched, and released. Towing mechanisms are located on the forward fuselage centerline. In preparing for target towing, ground personnel attach a tow target carrier or container to each of the Aero 15D racks. A release ring on the end of each tow line is attached to the towing mechanisms. During flight, the pilot energizes the armament bus and operates a tow target launch switch to stream the desired target. Following towing operations, the target is released by electrically opening the release mechanism through pilot operation of a target release switch. In the event that a tow line or target fouls during launch, the target can be released through use of the normal release or through either the bombing or rocket system controls. When the bombing system controls are selected and operated, the tow line release mechanism as well as the Aero 15D rack is actuated, dropping both the target container or carrier and the target. When the rocket system controls are selected and operated, only the target release system functions. In an emergency, both targets, the target containers and release rings are jettisoned through use of the stores jettison button.

ARMAMENT CONTROL SELECTOR

The Armament Control selector controls power routing to the bomb rack release shackles or bomb containers for bombing, to the rocket rails or pods during rocketry or to the gun packages during gunnery. The Armament Control selector positions operate the system as follows:

Selector Position	Fire or Release Selection
Off	None
Bombs-Sta 1	LH Bomb(s)
Sta 2	RH Bomb(s)
Sta 1 & Sta 2	LH and RH Bomb(s)
Rockets-	
Sta 1 & Sta 2	LH and RH Rocket(s)
Sta 2	RH Rocket(s)
Sta 1	LH Rocket(s)
Guns	Gun Pods

ROCKETS

For rocketry operations, air-to-air or air-to-ground, various rockets may be carried singly or in pods on the Aero 15D racks. Rockets may be fired from a single station, from both stations simultaneously, or they may be jettisoned (including the pods). When carrying rocket pods, the complete rocket pods may be dropped, if desired, in the same manner as a bomb, provided that ordnance personnel have positioned the wheel well bomb selector switches to SINGLE.

FIRE CONTROL SYSTEM (AN/AWG-6)

The AN/AWG-6 fire control system is composed of the following equipment:

Ranging Radar Set (AN/AWG-30A)
Aircraft Fire Control System (MK 6 Mod 4)
Gun-Bomb-Rocket Sight (MK 8 Mod 9)
Sight Control (MK 20 Mod 0)

This system is used with the aircraft armament system to accomplish delivery of ordnance of training. The system is capable of accepting radar or manual target range data for aerial gunnery or rocketry, or mechanically adjusted range and dive angle data for delivery of bombs, rockets and gunfire on ground targets. Radar or manual range information is relayed to the MK6 AFCS, which presents corrected aiming data to the pilot through the MK 8 Mod 9 sight.

RANGING RADAR (AN/APG-30A)

The ranging radar generates electronic pulses in a cone approximately 18 degrees in diameter. Radiated energy is reflected by a target (aircraft or reflector), returned to the set through the antenna and directed to a range data converter. The converter generates a d-c voltage proportional to the time interval between pulse generation and detection of the reflected energy. Since velocity of energy transmitted in space is constant for a given pressure altitude, the time interval is directly proportional to range. The d-c voltage generated by the range data converter is sent to the MK 6 AFCS as range-to-target.

RADAR LOCK-ON

If no target capable of reflecting radiated energy is present within the energy cone, the set continuously sweeps to maximum range and back. When a target is detected, the reflected energy, besides being processed into range voltage, is directed to a range tracking circuit, which locks onto the detected target. If the target is moved out of the radar search cone, the tracking circuit will break lock, causing the radar to sweep its operating range until a new target is detected. Radar operating range is 675 to 9000 feet. The MK 6 Mod 4 AFCS, however, limits radar range to approximately 2400 feet to minimize lock-on interference from ground targets.

AIRCRAFT FIRE CONTROL SYSTEM (MK 6 MOD 4)

The AFCS accepts radar range input and establishes control voltages for the sight unit during air-to-air gunnery or rocketry. In addition, the system generates range tones, which are transmitted through the intercom to the pilots. When the radar locks on a target, a 400-cycle tone is heard. At a preset maximum openfire distance, the tone frequency changes to 800 cycles, and returns to 400 cycles at a predetermined breakoff range. The AFCS range data converter sends a voltage in proportion to range to the gyro unit of the MK 8 Mod 9 sight. This voltage forces a controlled precession of the gyro, moving the gyro image. This movement establishes an angle of lead providing a continuous tracking solution for air-to-air gunnery or rocketry.

GUN/BOMB/ROCKET SIGHT (MK 8 MOD 9)

The MK 8 Mod 9 sight unit is a gyrostabilized, lead-computing, reflecting sight which provides an offset sight line having the proper lead angle for aiming fixed, forward-firing armament. The sight has both fixed and movable reticle image projection systems. Both reticles are projected through a seperate collimating lens onto a reflector plate, presenting the images as though superimposed. The fixed reticle image may be divided into two seperate patterns, while the gyro reticle image is a circle formed by the tips of six diamonds with a center pipper.

T-2 ATTACK KIT AS USED ON THE T-2E

In addition to its role as a trainer, the T-2 is an excellent light attack aircraft. A highly flexible weapons delivery capability is provided by factory or field-installed accessory kits. The kits include an armament package to equip six store stations; reticulated foam for all fuel tanks; a self-sealing main fuselage tank; an armament control panel; and a gun/bomb sight. With the stores accessory kit installed, both inboard stations are configured for gun pod installation. Multiple armament arrangements can be carried on any of the six store stations. Rocket or bomb combinations of up to 750 pounds may be carried on each inboard station and up to 500 pounds may be loaded on the intermediate and outboard stations. A total weapons capacity of 3500 pounds is available for use in the light attack role.

AERIAL GUNNERY PATTERN

The "Squirrel-cage" gunnery pattern may be likened roughly to a circle. The four firing aircraft move around on the periphery of this circle, equally seperated, 90 degrees apart. The tow aircraft and banner constitute a small chord at one side of the circle, with the starting or perch position on the opposite side. The plane of the circle is inclined to the horizontal by the amount of altitude advantage of the perch position above the tow aircraft and banner. This circle moves along relative to the speed and direction of the tow aircraft

MARK 8 MOD 9 SIGHT UNIT

GUN/BOMB/ROCKET SIGHT

22. MANUAL RANGE KNOB
23. TARGET SPAN LEVER
24. FIXED RETICLE MASKING LEVER
25. COLIMATING LENSES
26. GUN CAMERA ERECTOR
27. VARIABLE REFLECTOR KNOB
28. ID-295/APG-30 TRACKING INDICATOR
29. RANGE METER
30. ON-TARGET LIGHT
31. AFC METER (CRYSTAL CURRENT)
32. KB-9A GUN CAMERA

T-2 Accessory Kit Stores Capability

Store	Stations 1/6	2/5	3/4	Weight (Lbs.)
Gun Pods				
GPU-3A			–	180
Low Drag Bombs				
MK 81	–	–	–	260
MK 82	–	–	–	531
M-117AL			–	823
Retarded Bombs				
MK 81 Snakeye	–	–	–	305
MK 82 Snakeye I	–	–	–	560
M 117			–	857
Flare Dispensers				
SUU-40/A	–		–	327
SUU-44/A	–		–	350
Rocket Packages				
LAU-3A	–	–	–	427
LAU-32/A	–	–	–	175
LAU-10/A	–	–	–	533
LAU-69/A	–	–	–	507
LAU-68/A	–	–	–	218
LAU-67/A	–	–	–	175
Fire Bombs				
MK 77 Mod 2	–	–	–	520
BLU-1/B	–			712
BLU-27/B	–			847
BLU-10/B	–	–	–	250
(unfinned)				

GUN CAMERA (KB-9A)

The gun camera unit is mounted on an adapter plate on the sight unit. The camera utilizes a 35-foot pack of 16mm motion picture film and records sight pictures when the ARMT MASTER switch is at ON and the gun-rocket trigger is depressed or when the CAMERA TEST switch is held in TEST. The aperture may be set from f/3.5 to f/16 to compensate for varying light conditions. A thermostat and heater in the camera lens mount operate when the camera is running.

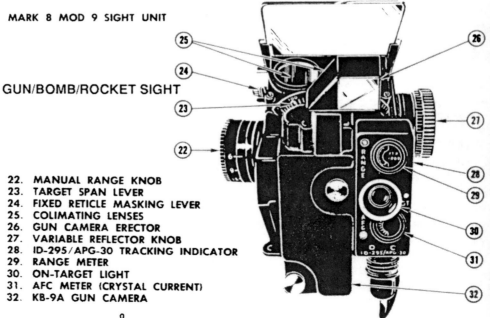

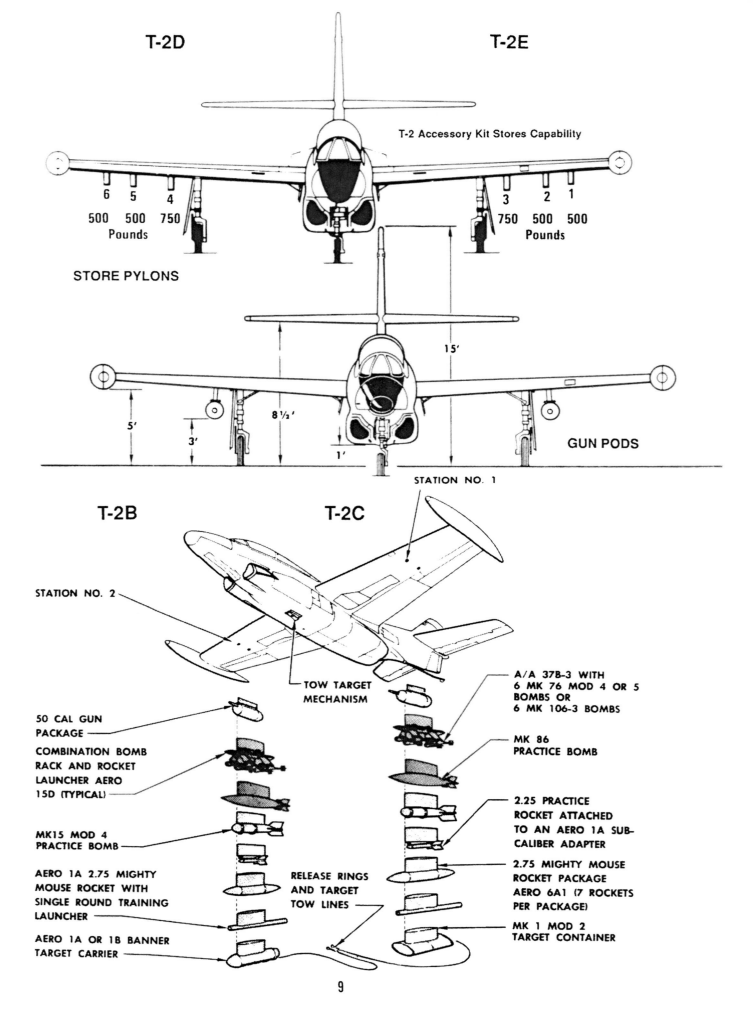

T-2D

T-2E

T-2 Accessory Kit Stores Capability

6 5 4

500 500 750
Pounds

STORE PYLONS

3 2 1

750 500 500
Pounds

15'

5'

3'

8½'

1'

GUN PODS

STATION NO. 1

T-2B

T-2C

STATION NO. 2

TOW TARGET
MECHANISM

50 CAL GUN
PACKAGE

COMBINATION BOMB
RACK AND ROCKET
LAUNCHER AERO
15D (TYPICAL)

MK15 MOD 4
PRACTICE BOMB

AERO 1A 2.75 MIGHTY
MOUSE ROCKET WITH
SINGLE ROUND TRAINING
LAUNCHER

AERO 1A OR 1B BANNER
TARGET CARRIER

RELEASE RINGS
AND TARGET
TOW LINES

A/A 37B-3 WITH
6 MK 76 MOD 4 OR 5
BOMBS OR
6 MK 106-3 BOMBS

MK 86
PRACTICE BOMB

2.25 PRACTICE
ROCKET ATTACHED
TO AN AERO 1A SUB-
CALIBER ADAPTER

2.75 MIGHTY MOUSE
ROCKET PACKAGE
AERO 6A1 (7 ROCKETS
PER PACKAGE)

MK 1 MOD 2
TARGET CONTAINER

9

CONFIGURATION

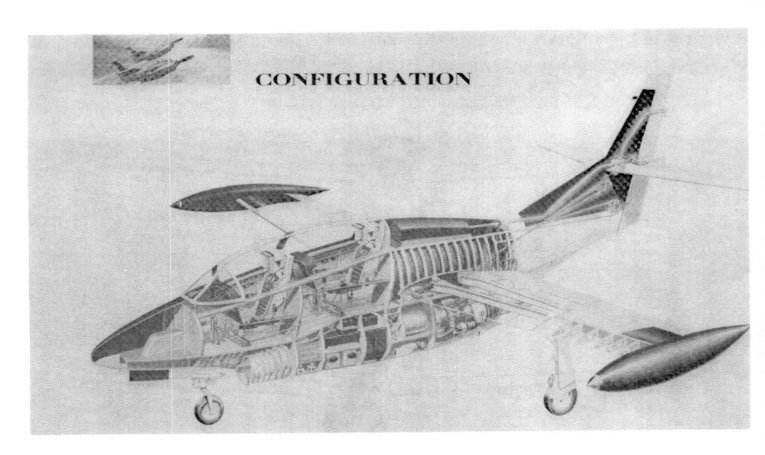

T-2C instrument panel, note the pencilled 314 in the lower right hand corner and the 14 above the "ball", that was done by pilots so they could remember the nose number for radio calls. The crossed out 58 was the nose number when this T-2C was a gun bird. (USN via T. Goldstone)

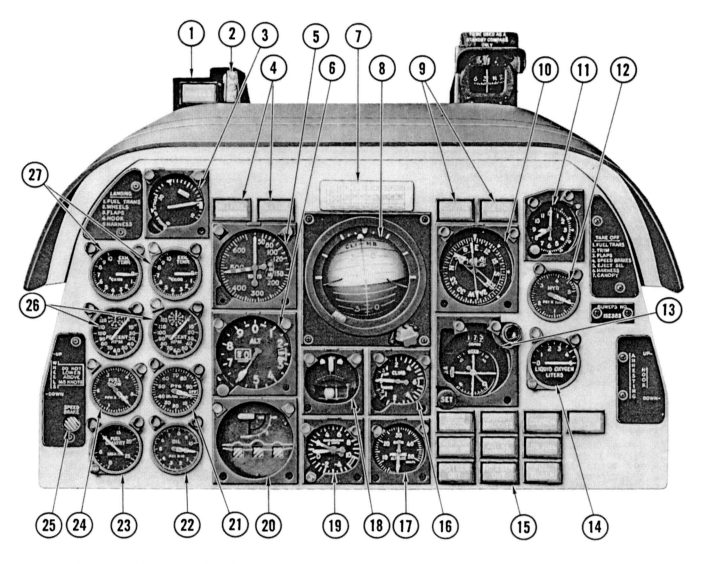

1. WHEELS WARNING LIGHT
2. APPROACH INDEXER
3. ANGLE-OF-ATTACK INDICATOR
4. NO. 1 ENGINE FIRE WARNING LIGHTS
5. AIRSPEED INDICATOR
6. ALTIMETER
7. AIRSPEED CORRECTION CARD
8. VERTICAL GYRO INDICATOR
9. NO. 2 ENGINE FIRE WARNING LIGHTS
10. BEARING-DISTANCE-HEADING INDICATOR
11. CLOCK
12. HYDRAULIC PRESSURE INDICATOR
13. TACAN COURSE INDICATOR
14. LIQUID OXYGEN QUANTITY INDICATOR
15. CAUTION LIGHTS
16. RATE-OF-CLIMB INDICATOR
17. CABIN PRESSURE ALTIMETER
18. TURN AND SLIP INDICATOR
19. ACCELEROMETER
20. LANDING GEAR AND FLAP POSITION INDICATOR
21. PT5 PRESSURE INDICATOR
22. OIL PRESSURE INDICATOR
23. FUEL QUANTITY INDICATOR
24. FUEL FLOW INDICATOR
25. SPEED BRAKE INDICATOR
26. TACHOMETERS
27. EXHAUST GAS TEMPERATURE INDICATORS

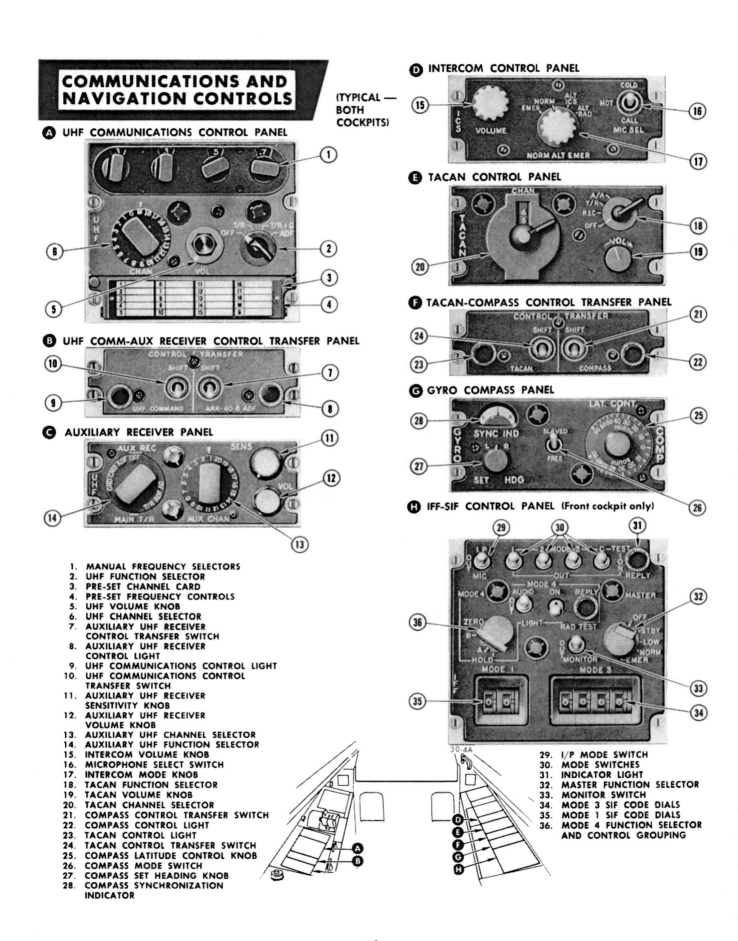

COMMUNICATIONS AND NAVIGATION CONTROLS

(TYPICAL — BOTH COCKPITS)

A UHF COMMUNICATIONS CONTROL PANEL

B UHF COMM-AUX RECEIVER CONTROL TRANSFER PANEL

C AUXILIARY RECEIVER PANEL

D INTERCOM CONTROL PANEL

E TACAN CONTROL PANEL

F TACAN-COMPASS CONTROL TRANSFER PANEL

G GYRO COMPASS PANEL

H IFF-SIF CONTROL PANEL (Front cockpit only)

1. MANUAL FREQUENCY SELECTORS
2. UHF FUNCTION SELECTOR
3. PRE-SET CHANNEL CARD
4. PRE-SET FREQUENCY CONTROLS
5. UHF VOLUME KNOB
6. UHF CHANNEL SELECTOR
7. AUXILIARY UHF RECEIVER
   CONTROL TRANSFER SWITCH
8. AUXILIARY UHF RECEIVER
   CONTROL LIGHT
9. UHF COMMUNICATIONS CONTROL LIGHT
10. UHF COMMUNICATIONS CONTROL
    TRANSFER SWITCH
11. AUXILIARY UHF RECEIVER
    SENSITIVITY KNOB
12. AUXILIARY UHF RECEIVER
    VOLUME KNOB
13. AUXILIARY UHF CHANNEL SELECTOR
14. AUXILIARY UHF FUNCTION SELECTOR
15. INTERCOM VOLUME KNOB
16. MICROPHONE SELECT SWITCH
17. INTERCOM MODE KNOB
18. TACAN FUNCTION SELECTOR
19. TACAN VOLUME KNOB
20. TACAN CHANNEL SELECTOR
21. COMPASS CONTROL TRANSFER SWITCH
22. COMPASS CONTROL LIGHT
23. TACAN CONTROL LIGHT
24. TACAN CONTROL TRANSFER SWITCH
25. COMPASS LATITUDE CONTROL KNOB
26. COMPASS MODE SWITCH
27. COMPASS SET HEADING KNOB
28. COMPASS SYNCHRONIZATION
    INDICATOR

29. I/P MODE SWITCH
30. MODE SWITCHES
31. INDICATOR LIGHT
32. MASTER FUNCTION SELECTOR
33. MONITOR SWITCH
34. MODE 3 SIF CODE DIALS
35. MODE 1 SIF CODE DIALS
36. MODE 4 FUNCTION SELECTOR
    AND CONTROL GROUPING

30-4A

LEFT CONSOLE

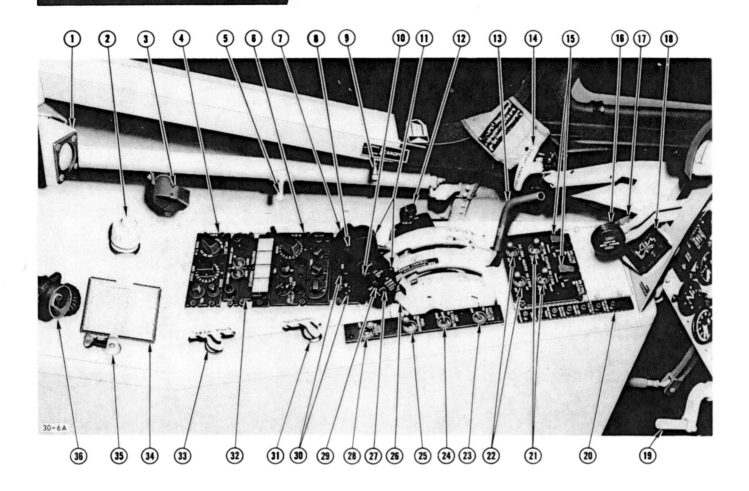

1. THUNDERSTORM LIGHT
2. ANTI-G SUIT VALVE
3. CONSOLE FLOODLIGHT
4. AUXILIARY UHF RECEIVER CONTROL PANEL
5. AIR DEFLECTOR CONTROL
6. UHF COMMUNICATIONS CONTROL PANEL
7. POWER CONTROL LEVERS
8. RUDDER TRIM SWITCH
9. CANOPY SWITCH
10. MICROPHONE SWITCH
11. POWER CONTROL LEVER RELEASE BUTTONS ●
12. FLAP HANDLE
13. CATAPULT HOLD HANDLE
14. CANOPY EMERGENCY RELEASE HANDLE
15. AIR START SWITCHES
16. LANDING GEAR HANDLE
17. LANDING GEAR HYDRAULIC SYSTEM OVERRIDE SWITCH ▲
18. NO. 1 VOLTAMMETER

19. RUDDER PEDAL ADJUST CRANK
20. CIRCUIT-BREAKER PANEL ▲
21. START SWITCHES
22. ENGINE MASTER SWITCHES ▲
23. EXTERIOR LIGHTS MASTER SWITCH
24. LANDING AND TAXI LIGHT SWITCH
25. FUEL TRANSFER SWITCH
26. POWER CONTROL LEVER FRICTION LEVER ▲
27. SIGHT SWITCH (GATES OUT) ▲
28. HYDRAULIC BOOST SWITCH ▲
29. SPEED BRAKE SWITCH
30. TRIM INDICATORS
31. SPEED BRAKE DUMP HANDLE ▲
32. UHF AND AUX RECEIVER CONTROL TRANSFER PANEL
33. TIP TANK FUEL DUMP HANDLE ▲
34. AUX RECEIVER CHANNEL CARD
35. OXYGEN ON-OFF HANDLE
36. EMERGENCY LIGHT

▲ FORWARD COCKPIT ONLY
● AFT COCKPIT ONLY

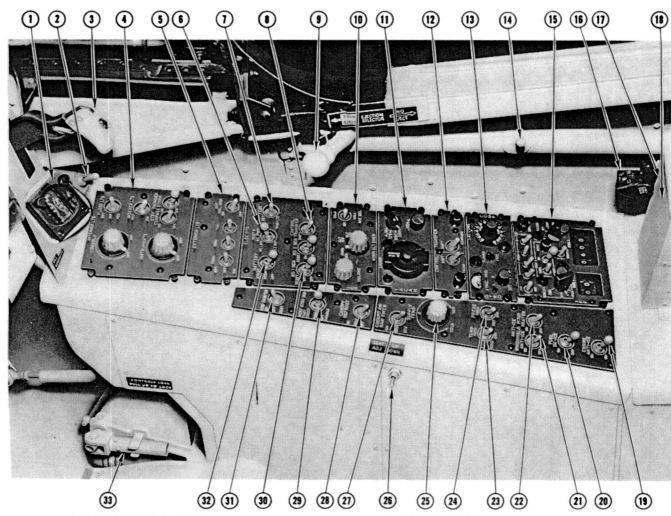

1. NO. 2 VOLT AMMETER
2. FIELD-CARRIER SWITCH ▲
3. ARRESTING HOOK HANDLE
4. INTERIOR LIGHTS
5. EXTERIOR LIGHTS CONTROL PANEL
6. INSTRUMENT A-C POWER SWITCH ▲
7. FIRE DETECTOR AND WARNING
   LIGHTS TEST SWITCH
8. CONTROL TRANSFER SHIFT SWITCH
9. EJECTION COMMAND SELECTOR HANDLE
10. INTERCOM CONTROL PANEL
11. TACAN CONTROL PANEL
12. TACAN-COMPASS CONTROL
    TRANSFER PANEL
13. MA-1 GYRO COMPASS CONTROL PANEL
14. AIR DEFLECTOR CONTROL
15. IFF-SIF CONTROL PANEL ▲
16. CONSOLE FLOODLIGHT
17. INSTRUMENT HOOD STOWAGE ●

18. DATA CASE
19. ENGINE ANTI-ICE SWITCH ▲
20. ENGINE FUEL DE-ICE SWITCH ▲
21. WINDSHIELD ANTI-ICE SWITCH ▲
22. PITOT HEATER SWITCH ▲
23. MANUAL TEMPERATURE SWITCH ▲
24. COCKPIT PRESSURE SWITCH ▲
25. SUPPLY AIR TEMPERATURE KNOB ▲
26. SEAT ADJUST SWITCH
27. RAM EMERGENCY SWITCH ▲
28. CANOPY DEFROST SWITCH
29. VERTICAL GYRO INDICATOR
    FAST ERECT SWITCH
    AFT COCKPIT DISABLE ▲
30. GENERATOR SWITCHES
31. YAW DAMPER SWITCH
32. BATTERY SWITCH ▲
    EMERGENCY DISCONNECT SWITCH ●
33. CONTROL LOCK HANDLE ▲

▲ FORWARD COCKPIT ONLY
● AFT COCKPIT ONLY

SERVICING

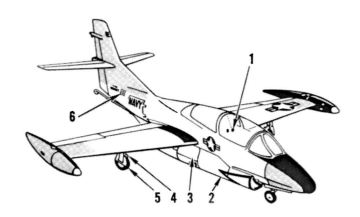

SPECIFICATIONS

FUEL JP-4 OR JP-5	(MIL-J-5624)
OIL	MIL-L-23699 (WEP)
HYDRAULIC FLUID	MIL-H-5606 (RED)
LIQUID OXYGEN	MIL-O-21749 (WEP)

CANOPY PNEUMATIC JETTISONING FILLER (VIEWED FROM LEFT SIDE)

PRECHARGE 2800—3200 PSI

LIQUID OXYGEN SYSTEM FILLER VALVE

CAPACITY — 5 LITERS

HYDRAULIC RESERVOIR FILLER

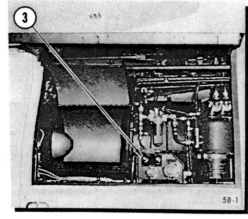

1.1 GALLONS

TIRE PRESSURES (TYPICAL)
(ON LANDING GEAR STRUTS)

MAIN GEAR TIRE, FILLER VALVE & SLIPPAGE MARK

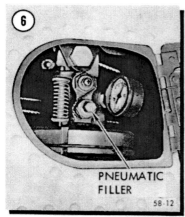

ARRESTING HOOK SNUBBER PRECHARGE — 600 PSI

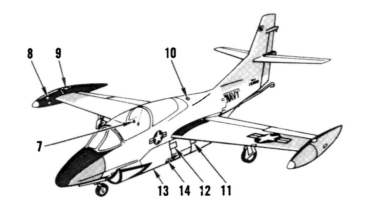

ENGINE STARTING UNITS	
ELECTRICAL **POWER UNITS**	
USN	USAF
NC-5, -7C, -10, -12 NA-5	A-3, -3A, -7 C-22, -26 MA-1MP, -2MP, -3MP MD-3, -3A

WHEEL BRAKE
RESERVOIR
(1 QUART)

TIP TANK
SIGHT
GLASSES

GRAVITY FUEL FILLER
TIP TANK (TYPICAL)
CAPACITY — 102 GALLONS

FUSELAGE TANK GRAVITY
FUEL FILLER
CAPACITY — 387 GALLONS

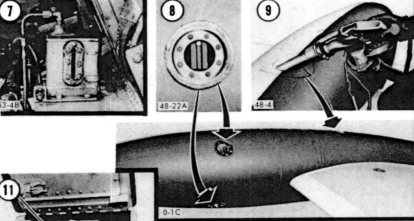

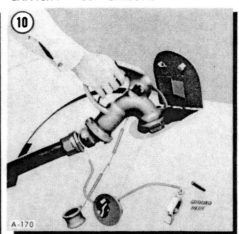

OIL FILLER
SERVICE THIS AIRCRAFT
WITH MIL-L-23699 OIL

OIL TANK FILLER (TYP)
1.5 GALLONS

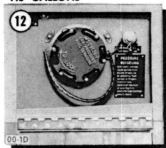

SINGLE-POINT REFUELING
RECEPTACLE 591 GALLONS

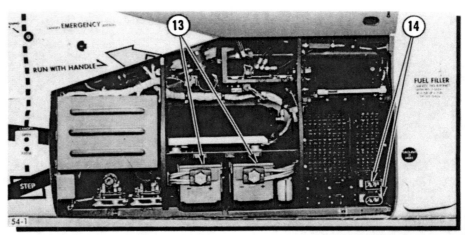

BATTERIES   EXTERNAL POWER
                           RECEPTACLES

EXTERIOR INSPECTION

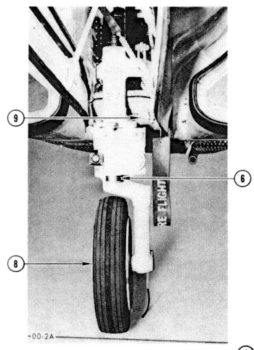

-00-2A-

NOSE SECTION

1. Pitot cover removed, airstream direction detector uncovered.
2. Landing and taxi light retracted.
3. Port and starboard duct plugs removed and ducts unobstructed.
4. Radar/baggage compartment door secure. (Radar/baggage compartment equipment secure.*)
5. Check shimmy damper indicator rod.
6. Check nose gear strut for extension—3 ½ inches hydraulic leaks and snap back action of nose gear tie-down rings.
7. Check nose wheel tire for wear, inflation and slippage.
8. Check nose wheel spindle safety pin removed.
9. Nose gear safety pin removed, safety lock handle latched.*

00-1M

PORT EQUIPMENT BAY AND FUSELAGE AREA

37. Check inlet duct for foreign objects through engine inspection door. Secure door.
38. Fuel and oil caps secure. Access doors secure.
39. Prior to all catapult launches, check catapult holdback fitting for visual defects and freedom of movement.
40. Check batteries secure; connections tight.*
41. Equipment secure; circuit breakers in.*
42. Access and equipment bay doors secure; all duct plugs removed; check area for hydraulic leaks.
43. Static port clear.
44. Check exterior canopy release handle flush.

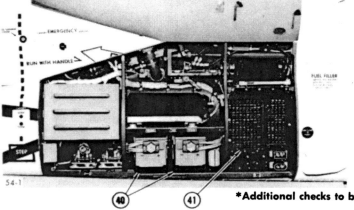

54-1

PORT WHEEL WELL AND WING

30. Check wing, aileron and flap for condition and security.
31. Check tip tank fuel level.
32. Check exterior lights undamaged.
33. Check main gear strut for extension — 3 ¼ inches, check integrity of scissors bolt, hydraulic leaks and snap back action of main gear tie-down rings. (Gear safety pin removed.*)
34. Check boost pump test switch — OFF. Arm Safety Disable switch — NORM and Tail Hook By-pass switch — NORM and all switch guards closed.
35. Check condition of brake pucks.
36. Check tire for wear, inflation and slippage; main wheel chocked. Inboard landing gear door open.

*Additional checks to be carried out prior to cross-country flight.   T-2B-1-00-8B

STARBOARD EQUIPMENT BAY AND FUSELAGE AREA

10. Static port clear.
11. Check wheel brake reservoir fluid level.
12. Inspection access and equipment bay doors secure. (Equipment secure; check fuses.*)
13. Check inlet duct for foreign objects through compressor inspection access door. Secure access door.
14. Check hydraulic power system reservoir fluid level.*
15. Hydraulic filler and ground test connections capped.*
16. Engine oil filler caps and access door — Secure.

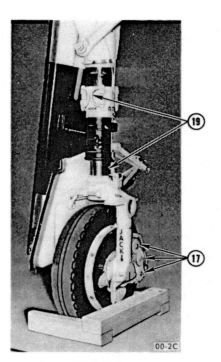

AFT FUSELAGE AND EMPENNAGE

23. Access and engine bay doors secure all duct plugs removed.
24. Check engine bay area for fuel and hydraulic leaks.
25. Check speed brakes for hydraulic leaks and security.
26. Tail-pipe plugs removed; inspect tail-pipes and turbines for cracks, distortion, hot streaks and signs of damage.
27. Check arresting hook for hydraulic leaks and proper stowage.
28. Check arresting hook snubber pressure — 600 psi (hook up).
29. Fuel vent clear; exterior lights undamaged.

STARBOARD WHEEL WELL AND WING

17. Check condition of brake pucks.
18. Check tire for wear, inflation and slippage; main wheel chocked. Inboard landing gear door open.
19. Check main gear strut for extension — 3¼ inches, check integrity of scissors bolt, hydraulic leaks and snap back action of main gear tie-down rings. (Gear safety pin removed.*)
20. Check wing, aileron and flap for condition and security.
21. Check tip tank fuel level.
22. Check exterior lights undamaged.

T-2C

JET TRAINER

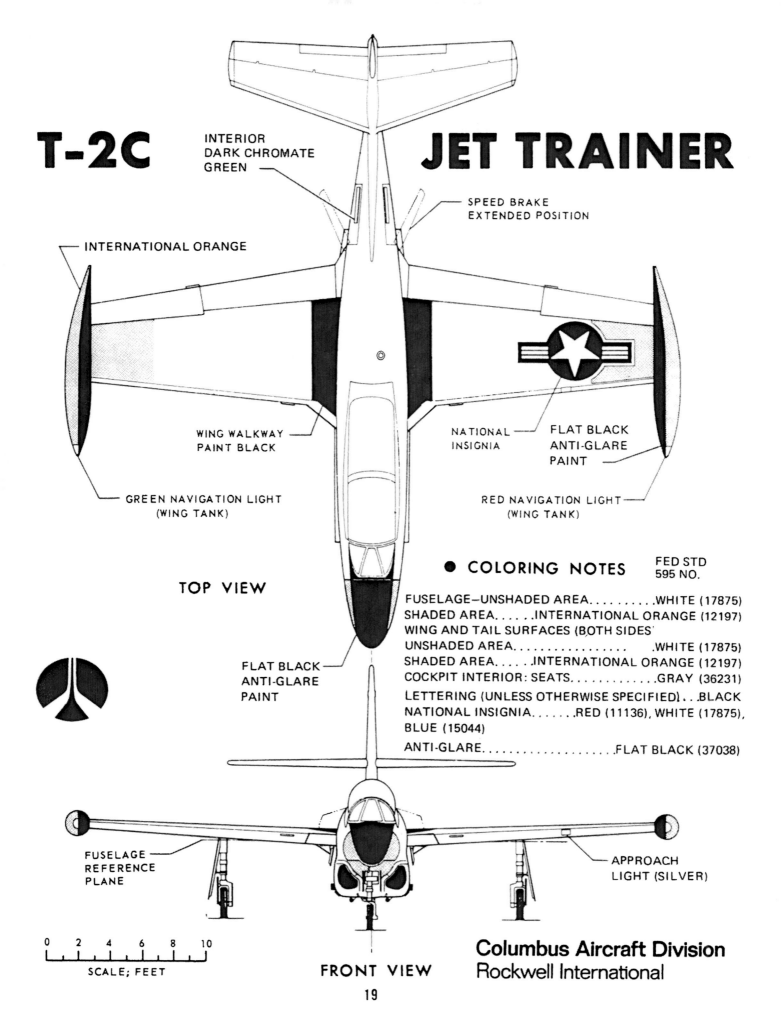

INTERIOR DARK CHROMATE GREEN

SPEED BRAKE EXTENDED POSITION

INTERNATIONAL ORANGE

WING WALKWAY PAINT BLACK

NATIONAL INSIGNIA

FLAT BLACK ANTI-GLARE PAINT

GREEN NAVIGATION LIGHT (WING TANK)

RED NAVIGATION LIGHT (WING TANK)

TOP VIEW

FLAT BLACK ANTI-GLARE PAINT

● COLORING NOTES

FED STD 595 NO.

FUSELAGE—UNSHADED AREA.........WHITE (17875)
SHADED AREA.....INTERNATIONAL ORANGE (12197)
WING AND TAIL SURFACES (BOTH SIDES)
UNSHADED AREA..................WHITE (17875)
SHADED AREA.....INTERNATIONAL ORANGE (12197)
COCKPIT INTERIOR: SEATS............GRAY (36231)
LETTERING (UNLESS OTHERWISE SPECIFIED)...BLACK
NATIONAL INSIGNIA......RED (11136), WHITE (17875), BLUE (15044)
ANTI-GLARE....................FLAT BLACK (37038)

FUSELAGE REFERENCE PLANE

APPROACH LIGHT (SILVER)

FRONT VIEW

Columbus Aircraft Division
Rockwell International

19

SECTION A
SECTION B
SECTION C

ARRESTING HOOK
(PAINT ALTERNATE
BLACK & WHITE
BANDS)

ANTI-COLLISION LIGHT
(WHITE)

SECTION D

SECTION E

CATAPULT
HOOK

HOLDBACK
FITTING

NAVY

FUSELAGE CROSS SECTIONS

SECTION F
SECTION G
SECTION H

BOTTOM VIEW

SECTION J
SECTION K
SECTION L

ANTI-COLLISION
LIGHT
(RED)

RED "WARNING" DECALS
(BOTH SIDES)

FORMATION LIGHT
(WING TANK)
LH-RED, RH-GREEN

FUSELAGE
FORMATION LIGHT
(YELLOW)

A B C D   E F   G   H   J   K   L

FUSELAGE
REFERENCE
PLANE

PITOT
TUBE

LANDING &
TAXI LIGHT
(RETRACTED)

STATIC DECK LINE

155239
1%

NAVY

AFT
POSITION
LIGHT
(WHITE)

WHITE BACKGROUND
RED LETTERS "DANGER"

RED STRIPE, WHITE LETTERS
"JET INTAKE" (BOTH SIDES)

LEFT SIDE VIEW
(RIGHT SIDE SIMILAR)

20

EJECTION SEAT

An LS-1 ejection seat is installed in each cockpit. See figure 1-8. This seat contains the controls and equipment necessary for ejection at any speed and altitude from a minimum of 75 knots at ground level. On aircraft 159721 and subsequent and aircraft having AFC 172, LS-1A ejection seats provide improved safe escape capability under conditions of low airspeed and altitude, or adverse altitudes, dive angles and sink rates by incorporating decreased time delays from initiation of the escape system to parachute inflation. An airspeed of 75 knots is required for safe ejection to avoid potential interference of seat and aircraft trajectories.

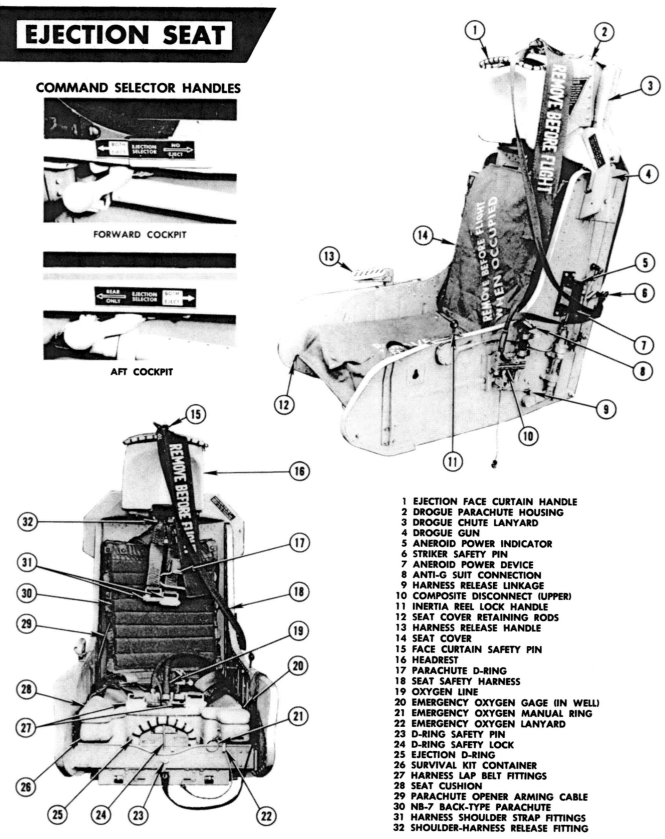

EJECTION SEAT

COMMAND SELECTOR HANDLES

FORWARD COCKPIT

AFT COCKPIT

1 EJECTION FACE CURTAIN HANDLE
2 DROGUE PARACHUTE HOUSING
3 DROGUE CHUTE LANYARD
4 DROGUE GUN
5 ANEROID POWER INDICATOR
6 STRIKER SAFETY PIN
7 ANEROID POWER DEVICE
8 ANTI-G SUIT CONNECTION
9 HARNESS RELEASE LINKAGE
10 COMPOSITE DISCONNECT (UPPER)
11 INERTIA REEL LOCK HANDLE
12 SEAT COVER RETAINING RODS
13 HARNESS RELEASE HANDLE
14 SEAT COVER
15 FACE CURTAIN SAFETY PIN
16 HEADREST
17 PARACHUTE D-RING
18 SEAT SAFETY HARNESS
19 OXYGEN LINE
20 EMERGENCY OXYGEN GAGE (IN WELL)
21 EMERGENCY OXYGEN MANUAL RING
22 EMERGENCY OXYGEN LANYARD
23 D-RING SAFETY PIN
24 D-RING SAFETY LOCK
25 EJECTION D-RING
26 SURVIVAL KIT CONTAINER
27 HARNESS LAP BELT FITTINGS
28 SEAT CUSHION
29 PARACHUTE OPENER ARMING CABLE
30 NB-7 BACK-TYPE PARACHUTE
31 HARNESS SHOULDER STRAP FITTINGS
32 SHOULDER-HARNESS RELEASE FITTING

In the Spring of 1970 under the joint sponsorship of NASA and the Naval Air Systems Command, North American was awarded a contract to test the supercritical wing concept on a T-2C. The supercritical wing is designed to avoid transonic drag and is thicker than the standard production wing and features a flattened rather than curved upper surface. The test wing was built-up from the T-2C's normal 12 percent thickness to 17 percent. The Buckeye's wing arrangement permitted engineers to alter the existing wing contour without any change to the fuselage or aircraft systems, including the retracting landing gear. A standard production T-2C wing was modified by the addition of balsa wood and fiber glass to obtain the desired thickness and configuration. By applying the supercritical principle to the Columbus-built T-2C aircraft, a direct comparison can be made between a production line aircraft and the same type aircraft with a supercritical airfoil.

T-2C SUPERCRITICAL WING

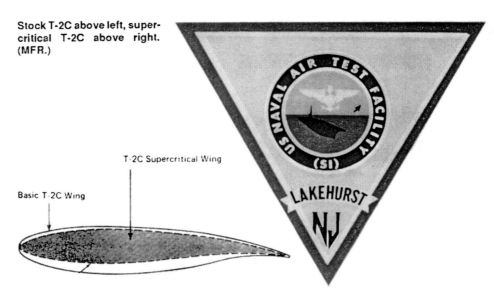

Stock T-2C above left, supercritical T-2C above right. (MFR.)

T-2C Supercritical Wing

Basic T-2C Wing

NT-2A 147432 assigned to NATF Lakehurst for catapult and arresting gear equipment testing in May 1965. (Clay Jansson) Colors are white and da-glo with tail stripes being black, white, red-orange, white and black.

YT2J-1 146001 of the System Test division of the Naval Air Test Center in 1960. The da-glo is extremely faded and notice the early style fore and aft, red intake chevrons and the styleized "S" on the tail. (Sommerich via Jansson)

YT2J-1 147432 assigned to NATC Patuxent River, Maryland. Note the blackened lower fuselage aft of the exhaust. (Peter Bowers via Besecker)

YT-2A 147433 assigned to Systems Test with styleized "S" on the tail and NATC below the horizontal stabilizer. (R.C. Seely via Menard)

U.S. NAVAL TEST PILOT SCHOOL

T-2C 158326, nose number 22, of the U.S. Naval Test Pilot School in 1980. Note Test Pilot School (TPS) insignia on the tail. (Werner Hartman)

T-2C 158579 of the TPS at NAS Patuxent River in 1982. Note the canvas intake covers. (Jim Burridge) YT-2B 144218 of the Naval Air Development Center on 5-19-73. Tail insignia is a black circle with NADC in da-glo red on a styleized gold NL, also note da-glo red gear door. (via Besecker)

Test Pilot School insignia

T-2C 158333 of the Naval Air Development Center on 6-19-77, with yellow and black test can attached to the nose test instrument boom, note white NADC on a styleized black tail arrow. (R.J. Pickett via Menard)

NAVAL AIR DEVELOPMENT CENTER

T-2B 152442 assigned to Headquarters U.S. Marine Corps, Washington D.C. A number of these aircraft were assigned so that Washington area Naval Aviators could stay current. Colors are white and red trim. (1976 via Burger)

T-2B 155224 of HQ USMC Washington on 5-20-76. Colors are white with a gold-brown   vertical tail,   tip tanks and   lower foreward fuselage. Nose to tail fuselage stripe is red. (B. Trombecky via Tailhook Photo Service VT 0194)

T2J-1 147494 used to keep Naval Aviators proficient at the Naval Post Graduate School, Montery, Calif., on 7-8-61. (Swisher)

Montery based T2J-1 147495 in March 1961, note da-glo wings with white control surfaces and natural metal leading edges. (CDR. Jack Bradford via Tailhook Photo Service VT-0516)

NAVAL POST GRADUATE SCHOOL

T2J-1 146009 of the Naval Air Technical Training Unit (NATTU) Olathe, Kansas in 1960. Note NATTU OLATHE on rear fuselage. (D Englehardt via W.T. Larkins)

TRAINING SQUADRON FOUR
VT-4

On 1 May 1960 Basic Training Group Nine (BTG-9) was commissioned Training Squadron Four (VT-4) at NAS Pensacola, Florida, under the command of CDR. H. V. Weldon. The squadron's mission was to provide jet air-to-air gunnery and initial field and shipboard carrier qualification training using the T2J-1 aircraft. The gunnery phase included ten flights, of which four were live firing flights. The carrier qualification phase included ten airfield carrier landing practices and one at-sea hop. This last flight to the aircraft carrier consisted of two touch-and-go landings and four arrested landings followed by four catapult launches.

Two days after commissioning, the last T-2V student flight was made by 1 LT. R. Kaye, USMC., and on 9 May 1960, the first field mirror landing practice (FMLP) in the T2J-1 was made by a student. This first was followed by 2 LT. J. B. Hammond, USMC, becoming the first student to carrier qualify in a T2J-1 by landing on the USS Antietam (CVS-36) on 2 June 1960.

In the second half of 1962 the USS Antietam was replaced by the USS Lex-

A T2J-1 of Basic Training Group Nine BTG-9, the forerunner of VT-4, makes the 20,000 th. Catapult shot off the USS Antietam (CVS-36) in 1960. (USN via Tailhook)

ington (CVS-16) and on 2 July 1963 VT-4 had made its 1,000th. arrested landing on the "Blue Ghost". In September 1964 the "Lady Lex" departed for a six month overhaul period and VT-4 was forced to schedule carrier qualifications aboard available fleet carriers. Thusly, carrier qualifications were conducted aboard the following carriers:

17 Oct.63	USS Intrepid	(CVS-11)	off Pensacola
27 Oct.63	USS Essex	(CVS-9)	off Pensacola
4 Nov.63	USS Essex	(CVS-9)	off Pensacola
13 Dec.63	USS Shangra-La	(CVA-38)	off Mayport
15 Jan.64	USS Intrepid	(CVS-11)	off Mayport
23 Feb.64	USS Wasp	(CVS-18)	off Mayport
21 Mar.64	USS Essex	(CVS-9)	off Mayport
5 Apr.64	USS F.D.R.	(CVA-42)	off Mayport

In January 1970 the "Lady Lex" went into overhaul again and was temporaraly replaced by the USS Intrepid.

On 5 December 1965 VT-4 received the first T-2B "Buckeye" to replace its fleet of T2J-1s (redesignated T-2A in 1962). Ens. S. W. Means became the first VT-4 student to solo in the T-2B on 8 December 1966 and Ens. J. Millar, Jr. became the first carrier qualified T-2B student on 2 September 1966. In May of 1967, the last T-2A gunnery hop was flown and the last T-2A was mustered-out on 15 June 1967. The squadron began receiving the T-2C in May of 1970 and had phased out the T-2B by 1973.

From its inception in 1960 until March of 1971, VT-4 was assigned the unique primary mission of conducting jet air-to-air gunnery and initial carrier qualification training for all basic jet students. Thusly when students completed their transition training with VT-7 or VT-9 at NAS Meridian, Miss., They were assigned to VT-4. In March of 1971 the system of series flow was changed to parallel flow with four basic training squadrons (VT-4, 7, 9, and 19) providing essentially the same training. This training consisted of jet transition, precision aerobatics, basic-radio instruments, formation, night flying, air-to-air gunnery and carrier qualifications.

Another change in mission occurred in October 1972 when VT-4 was tasked with the dual mission of providing both transition (basic) and advanced jet training. The squadron primarily operated the T-2C and the TA-4J in this mission. Originally, however, the Grumman TF-9J "Cougar" was utilized as the advanced jet trainer, with the first F-9 flight taking place on 5 September 1972, followed by the first TA-4J flight on 12 November 1973. On 1 March 1974 the last F-9 was transferred out of the squadron. The first VT-4 students to be designated Naval Aviators under the new system, ENS. D. Jackson, ENS. K. Buchspics and LTJG J. Schott, were so designated on 9 May 1973.

Under a program initiated in 1973, VT-4 completed training and designated 22 Master of Science Naval Aviators in 1975. Also in 1975 the first flight surgeon class and Kuwaiti Air Force class was started at VT-4. The Kuwaiti Air Force training program concluded in 1980, however foreign student training continued with 17 Singapore students completed in 1981, 11 in 1982, 4 in 1983, 11 in 1984 and 9 in 1985. In addition 3 Spanish students were graduated in 1982, 2 in 1984 and 1 Indonesian student in 1985.

In 1985 the Squadron's mission once again changed. On 20 December 1985, VT-4 officially changed missions and became the E-2/C-2 training squadron for the Navy. The new E-2/C-2 syllabus consisted of 68 flights and 140.4 hours of academics. The flights were broken down to 4 basic instruments, 18 familiarization, 5 radio instruments, 17 formation, 7 airways navigation, 5 night familiarization and 12 carrier qualifications. In this new mission VT-4 utilized only the T-2C "Buckeye" and transferred its last TA-4J (158318) to VT-7 on 15 April 1986.

Throughout its history VT-4 has amassed numerous awards. These included the Captain's Cup in 1961, the Admiral's Efficiency cup in 1965, the Chief of Naval Operations Safety Award for 1961, 1962, 1965 and 1971, and the Chief of Naval Air Training Safety Award in 1972. But the most noteworthy award was the North American Aviation Safety Award for 3 1/2 years or 70,000 accident-free flying hours in the T-2 from October 1962 to May 1966.

VT-4

T-2A 147475 from VT-4 does a touch-and-go abroad the USS Lexington on 2-4-63. Note side number on the gear door and the zinc chromate interior of the dive brakes. (USN via Tailhook)

T-2A 147485 from VT-4 in August 1962. The paint has bleached out to the point where its impossible to tell the difference between the white and the da-glo. (W.J. Balogh, Sr. via Menard)

TRAINING AIR WINGS

In 1971 the single base training concept was initiated and six Training Air Wings were established. TAW-1 (VT-7, VT-9 and VT-19), TAW-2, (VT-23), TAW-3 (VT-26) & TAW-6 (VT-4 and VT-10).

T-2B 152441 gun bird frow VT-4 with a relatively clean gun pod. Gun pods carried single .30 cal. guns. Aircraft is returning to Sherman Field, Pensacola on 5-23-67. (Clay Jansson)

Another T-2B gun bird, 152451, with da-glo gun pods, on 5-23-67. Note VT-4 insignia on the nose.

The COs T-2B 155212 on 4-27-68. Rudder stripes are white, red, yellow, green and blue. (via Smalley)

VT-4 T-2C 157047 with Commander Training Air Wing Six written under NAVY on the fuselage, note the thin white outline surrounding the 2F on the tail. (Frad Roos, Naval Fighters)

T-2C 156687 from VT-4 with medium blue rudder stripes and yellow rescue arrow. Note more pronounced white around the 2F. (Fred Roos, Naval Fighters)

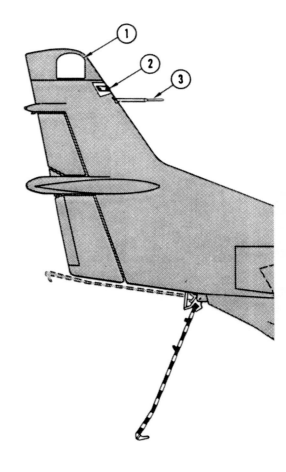

GENERAL ARRANGEMENT

TYPICAL

1. UHF COMM/TACAN ANTENNA
2. UPPER ANTI-COLLISION BEACON
3. AFT PITOT/STATIC TUBE
4. FORMATION LIGHT
5. FUSELAGE FUEL TANK
6. HYDRAULIC SYSTEM RESERVOIR
7. 2500 VA INVERTER
8. 750 VA INVERTER
9. RADAR/BAGGAGE COMPARTMENT
10. PITOT/TOTAL PRESSURE TUBE
11. LANDING AND TAXI LIGHT
12. A-C FUSE PANEL
13. VERTICAL GYRO (VGI)
14. MA-1 GYRO COMPASS AMPLIFIER
15. LIQUID OXYGEN SPHERE
16. AN/ARN-52 (TACAN) RECEIVER-TRANSMITTER
17. IFF TRANSPONDER, AN/APX-64
18. IFF TEST SET
19. CABIN CONDITIONING HEAT EXCHANGER
20. ENGINE OIL FILLER
21. AN/AWG-6 FIRE CONTROL SYSTEMS (PROVISIONS)
22. MARK 8 MOD 9 GUNSIGHT UNIT (PROVISIONS)
23. LS-1 (LS-1A) * EJECTION SEAT
24. STATIC PRESSURE PORT

* AIRCRAFT 159721 AND SUBSEQUENT AND AIRCRAFT
  HAVING AFC 172

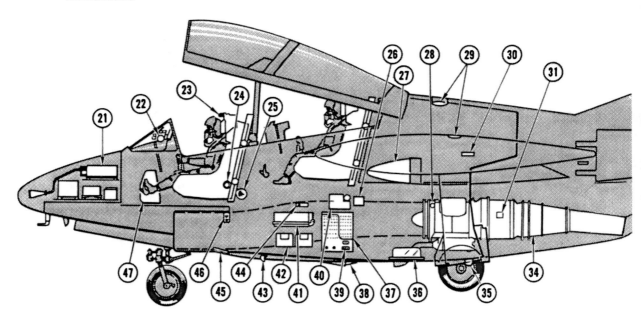

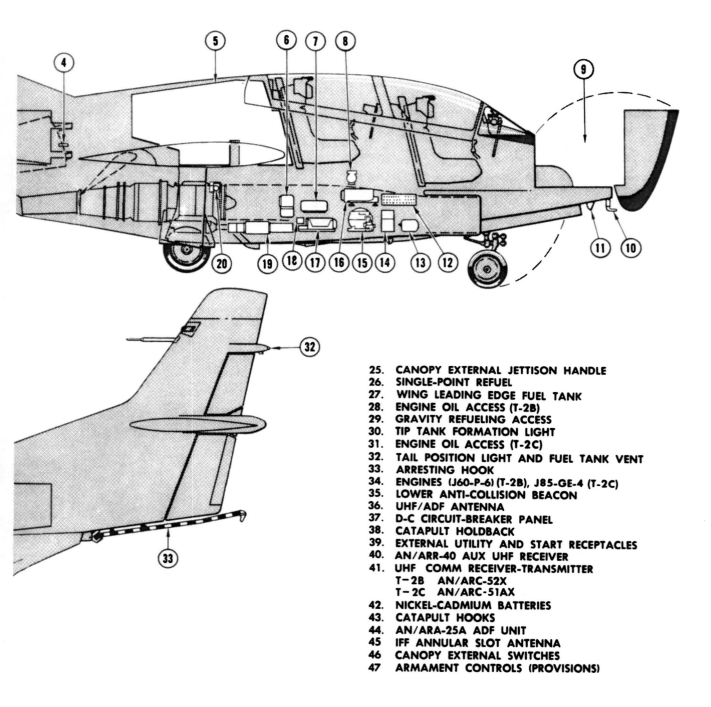

25. CANOPY EXTERNAL JETTISON HANDLE
26. SINGLE-POINT REFUEL
27. WING LEADING EDGE FUEL TANK
28. ENGINE OIL ACCESS (T-2B)
29. GRAVITY REFUELING ACCESS
30. TIP TANK FORMATION LIGHT
31. ENGINE OIL ACCESS (T-2C)
32. TAIL POSITION LIGHT AND FUEL TANK VENT
33. ARRESTING HOOK
34. ENGINES (J60-P-6) (T-2B), J85-GE-4 (T-2C)
35. LOWER ANTI-COLLISION BEACON
36. UHF/ADF ANTENNA
37. D-C CIRCUIT-BREAKER PANEL
38. CATAPULT HOLDBACK
39. EXTERNAL UTILITY AND START RECEPTACLES
40. AN/ARR-40 AUX UHF RECEIVER
41. UHF COMM RECEIVER-TRANSMITTER
    T-2B   AN/ARC-52X
    T-2C   AN/ARC-51AX
42. NICKEL-CADMIUM BATTERIES
43. CATAPULT HOOKS
44. AN/ARA-25A ADF UNIT
45 IFF ANNULAR SLOT ANTENNA
46 CANOPY EXTERNAL SWITCHES
47 ARMAMENT CONTROLS (PROVISIONS)

T-2C 156693 of VT-4 prior to a hop. Notice pilots gear hanging from the nose gear door and the inner main wheel door. (Fred Roos, Naval Fighters)

T-2C 159160 of VT-4 displaying its new single letter tail code "F", on 9-20-75. Note medium blue rudder stripes and the "F" on the gear door. (Clay Jansson)

T-2C 158876 from VT-4 with white nose numbers and "F" on the tail in November 1984. Note VT-4 insignia on the nose and black leading edges, rudder stripes and fin cap. (Bob Stollof)

TRAINING SQUADRON SEVEN VT-7

T2J-1 148159 from VT-7, note exhaust stains on the tail. (via Clay Jansson)

The origins of Training Squadron Seven can be traced back to the Naval Advanced Training Activity at NAS Memphis, Tenn. This activity, under the command of CDR. N. B. Hodson, was comprised of two Advanced Training Units: ATU-105 and ATU-205. ATU-105 and ATU-205 were consolidated into a single squadron, commissioned BTG-7, in July 1958, and transferred to the Basic Training Command while under the command of CDR. D. R. Flynn. The new squadron's mission was to train student Naval Aviators in basic instrument flying, utilizing the North American T-28 "Trojans" and Lockheed T2V Seastars".

In June 1960, while under the command of CDR. W. Roach, the squadron moved to NAS Kingsville, Texas, and began receiving the North American T2J-1 (T-2A) "Buckeye". In August of 1960, while under the command of CDR. R. F. Regan, the squadron was redesignated Training Squadron Seven (VT-7). With this new designation and the new T2J-1 aircraft, the squadron assumed its new mission of providing training in jet transition, precision aerobatics, basic and radio instruments, formation, gunnery and carrier qualifications.

VT-7 moved to its new permanent base, NAAS Meridian, Miss., in July of 1961. On 15 December 1961, VT-7 was split to form a "sister" squadron, VT-9, which had the same mission. When VT-7 was transferred to its new base, the gunnery and carrier qualification part of the syllabus was taken over by VT-4 at NAS Pensacola, Florida.

The basic T2J-1/T-2A flight training syllabus provided for 95 hours of flight instruction in the "Buckeye" trainer. The training was divided into six stages: transition, precision aerobatics, basic instruments, radio instruments, night familiarization and basic formation. In addition, 170 hours of ground training was provided in aerodynamics, flight support, meteorology, leadership and Naval organization. To accomplish this mission, VT-7 routinely operated 60 T2J-1/T-2A aircraft through 1965. During this period VT-7 was charged with a secondary mission of training "Basic Jet" flight instructors.

In August 1966, aircraft on hand were increased from 60 to 73 in response to the anticipated increases in student load created by the Southeast Asian crisis. Also in August, three twin-engine T-2B "Buckeyes" were assigned to the squadron for three months of testing and evaluation as training aircraft. During the initial testing of the T-2B in August, the squadron also tested the Air Force T-37B trainer for its suitability as a Naval basic trainer.

In 1967 the squadron's T-2A fleet was expanded to 85 aircraft in anticipation of a greater student load from the Vietnam War.

On 1 July 1968 the training syllabus changed to Phase A and Phase B, with VT-7 conducting Phase A training and VT-9 conducting Phase B training. Phase A consisted of 50.6 hours of T-2A jet transition, precision aerobatics, basic instruments, radio instruments and 180 hours of ground training. Phase B at VT-9 consisted of formation, night familiarization and transition to the new T-2B.

By the end of 1969 the number of T-2A aircraft increased to 109 because of the demand for new pilots created by the Vietnam conflict.

The T-2As began showing their age and hard use in 1969. A number of T-2As were sent to NARF, Pensacola, for repairs of cracks in the wings. A runaway trim problem associated with a 26 March 1969 crash was isolated in April and a program of reworked trim and stick assemblies was completed by July. After another accident on 2 July 1969, all T-2A aircraft were grounded because of repeated flameouts. The problem was corrected by removing the fuel controls and having NARF effect an upward adjustment of minimum fuel flow. The replacement was completed in August. In September, sixty-eight aircraft were flown to Pensacola for a main landing gear strut modification program which took seven weeks to complete.

In 1970 the squadron's T-2A fleet was augmented by the addition of the new T-2C aircraft. The first T-2C was received in November and a new one-squadron jet training program started immediately. The T-2C added formation and night transition training to the normal T-2A syllabus. The squadron finished 1970 with 72 T-2As and 14 T-2Cs.

In February 1971 VT-7 along with VT-9 changed their operating procedures from "series flow" to "parallel flow". Each squadron had the same syllabus and became responsible for their own carrier qualifications. A student was now able to complete basic jet training at a single base.

A change of mission occurred in October 1971 when VT-7 became the Advanced Training Squadron for NAS Meridian under the "singlebase" concept. On 14 October 1971, VT-7 flew its last student T-2 flight and on 15 October 1971 a formal "change of aircraft" ceremony was held. The new aircraft to be used in the advanced training syllabus was the McDonnell Douglas TA-4J Skyhawk, which is still in use today by VT-7.

In 1971 the T-2C count at VT-7 went from 14 in January to 46 in September with the change of mission at VT-7, and the T-2Cs were transferred to NAS Chase Field from October until 17 December 1971.

34

T-2A 148220 early orange da-glo scheme. (Jansson)

T-2A 146014. (R. Esposito)

T-2A 148184 in dark red-orange trim. (Roos, Naval Fighters)

T-2A 148177 on 6-15-68 with Efficency "E" on the nose. (Smalley)

T-2A 147474 from VT-7, note black shoe scuff marks on side of aircraft under the rescue arrow. (Fred Roos, Naval Fighters)

T-2A 148223 from VT-7 landing with half flaps and speedbrakes extended on 8-3-68. (Jim Sullivan via Besecker)

T-2C 157058 from VT-7 in 1971 with white 2K on tail outlined in black. The T-2C was only used from Oct. 1970 to Dec. 1971 at VT-7. (Fred Roos, Naval Fighters)

TRAINING SQUADRON NINE
VT-9

TIGER NINE

Training Squadron Nine was commissioned on Friday December 15, 1961, at the Naval Auxilliary Air Station, Meridian, Mississippi, with a core of personnel from its sister squadron VT-7. Since 1961, VT-9 has earned the nickname "Tiger Nine" by logging nearly 700,000 flight hours while graduating more than 6,300 Student Naval Aviators (through December 1986).

In 1966, with a strength of 68 T-2A "Buckeye" jet trainers, a new flight and maintenance scheduling plan was devised and instituted by VT-9's Commanding Officer, CDR. Thomas E. Davis. The plan, for which CDR. Davis received a letter of commendation from the Chief of Naval Air Basic Training,

increased pilot and aircraft utilization by over 50% and increased the jet student pilot training rate by 29%. The plan proved so successful that it was adopted by the other squadrons in the Basic Training Command.

Because of the escalation of the Viet Nam War and the projected need for more pilots the number of T-2As at VT-9 grew to 82 in 1967, and on June 6, 1968, the squadron's first T-2B arrived. On December 31, 1968, 59 T-2As and 21 T-2Bs were on hand. 1969 would bring the T-2C to the squadron on 30 April and by December 31st 45 T-2A, 19 T-2B and 43 T-2C aircraft were on hand. In 1970 the planned stocking of the squadron entirely with T-2Cs was reversed and by the end of the year 46 T-2As, 81 T-2Bs and 17 T-2Cs were assigned. By 15 March 1971, VT-9 had become the largest jet squadron in the Navy and on 2 August it was split into VT-9 and VT-19, with VT-9 retaining 17 T-2As and 38 T-2Bs for its mission. With the advent of VT-19, VT-9 picked up the additional duty of carrier qualification under the new parallel flow syllabus and relinquished its T-2As in early 1973.

In 1974 VT-9 instituted a 19 week jet transition syllabus for formerly Army trained Marine Corps helicopter pilots. In 1974 11 pilots were transitioned, 8 in 1975 and 5 in 1976. In 1977 and 1980 4 Spanish helicopter pilots underwent the transition training in preparation for the AV-8A Harrier. Also in 1977, 3 helicopter pilots were trained prior to posting at the Naval Test Pilot School.

1975 saw the advent of another transition program at VT-9, the S-3 transition

syllabus. 22 former prop pilots were transitioned in 1975, 18 in 1976, 5 in 1977, 2 in 1978, 3 in 1980, 2 in 1981, 4 in 1982 and 3 in 1984.

E2/C2 pilot training was acquired by VT-9 in 1982, with 4 pilots completing the course in 1982 and a high of 47 in 1984. VT-4 took over the E2/C2 training program from VT-9 on 20 December 1985.

The T-2C returned to the squadron in 1974 with December 31st showing 21 T2-Cs and 6 T-2Bs. The remaining T-2Bs were transferred out in 1975 and VT-9 finished the year with 25 T-2Cs, 22 in 1976, 18 in 1977, 18 in 1978, 18 in 1979, 19 in 1980, 21 in 1981, 21 in 1982, 21 in 1983, 24 in 1984, 24 in 1985 and 24 in 1986.

Training Squadron Nine is assigned to training Air Wing ONE. The mission of VT-9 is to train student Naval and Marine Corps Aviators in all phases of the intermediate strike jet syllabus. The syllabus includes aerobatics, basic and radio instruments, airways navigation, formation, night operations and carrier qualifications (CQ) utilizing the North-American Rockwell T-2C "Buckeye"aircraft. It should be noted that VT-9 specializes in the T-2C CQ phase of training for Training Air Wing ONE. VT-9 is the Model Manager for all T-2C "Buckeye" commands, which entails keeping abreast of all NATOPS Flight Manual changes, and disseminating this information to all commands operating the T-2C. VT-9 is also responsible for training all T-2C squadron NATOPS Check Pilots.

T-2A 148226 from VT-9 on 7-16-66, note black exhaust stain tail. (Clay Jansson)

T-2A 147490 of VT-9 with "Tiger Nine" insignia below the windscreen on 1-28-67. (Smalley)

T-2C 156686 of VT-9 on 6-13-69, note black bat which is painted below the "Tiger Nine" insignia. Note natural metal leading edge on tail. (Smalley)

COMMODORE N.R. GOODING JR. COMTRAWING ONE is written on the yellow nose placard of T-2B 153538 on 6-15-74. Tail stripes are red, white, blue. (Clay Jansson)

T-2C 156694 from VT-9 on 1-17-76 with new "A" tail code and USS Lexington painted on the fuselage. (Swisher)

TIGER NINE

T-2C 158593 of VT-9, note the nose number is repeated on the flaps. (Fred Roos, Naval Fighters)

T-2C 157054 of VT-9 in 1982 with "Tiger Nine" paw prints going over the fuselage. (via Burger)

TRAINING SQUADRON NINE
VT-9

T-2C 156723 from VT-9 in 1980, the paw prints are red and the stripes are red with black outlines.

TRAINING SQUADRON TEN VT-10

Training Squadron Ten (VT-10) was commissioned at Sherman Field, Pensacola, on 15 January 1968 when the Basic Naval Aviation Officer School was redesignated VT-10. The squadron was charged with two missions. The first was to provide basic academic and in-flight training for non-pilot aviation officers and officer candidates to prepare them for advanced training leading to eventual designation as Naval Flight Officers (NFO's). The second mission was to prepare students for advanced training leading to eventual designation as Air Intelligence Officers. To fullfill this mission VT-10 was equipped with eleven T-1A jet trainers and nine UC-45Js.

In 1970 the squadron's UC-45Js were replaced by the North American T-39D "Sabreliner" and in 1971 the T-1As were replaced by eight TF-9J "Cougars". Replacement of the "Cougars" started with the first delivery of the twin engined T-2B "Buckeye" on 16 October 1973. The first T-2B training flight took place on 24 October 1973 and the last "Cougar" training flight was on 18 December 1973 with the last F-9 being turned over to the Naval Aviation Museum at Pensacola on 28 December 1973.

With the influx of the modern T-39D and T-2B aircraft, as well as the new 1D23 communication and navigational ground trainer in 1972, VT-10's training syllabus was modified to include this new equipment.

Designed and built by General Electric, the 1D23 trainer includes forty individual cockpit stations which permit students to learn the aircraft navigation skills and radio communications tech-

niques required in the operation of typical Navy aircraft. Each station is capable of simulating a realistic operating environment with respect to aircraft flight performance, fuel consumption, radio communications and navigational systems. Typical fleet aircraft computer operations are also represented.

The aircraft instruments, controls and displays are controlled by a central digital computer, which activates each instrument to respond to student inputs as he navigates his "aircraft" over a pre-planned mission course. The system permits each student to direct his aircraft within a 1,024 by 1,024 mile problem area. The computer is capable not only of simulating flight situations, but also is able to record, evaluate and grade a student's performance throughout the mission.

With the implementation of this system, training efficiency is greatly increased by incorporating additional instruction into the NFO syllabus without a costly increase in actual flight hours.

July through Sept. 1975 would see the transition from the T-2B to the T-2C at VT-10. In July 13 T-2Cs were delivered and 9 T-2Bs were transferred, in August 12 T-2Cs were delivered and 8 T-2Bs were transferred, and in September one T-2C was delivered and 10 T-2Bs were transferred out.

At one point in the squadron's history, May 1976, the T-2C took over all U.S. student training activities when most of VT-10's T-39 fleet was grounded due to corrosion.

On March 15 1977, VT-10 submitted final drafts of a new basic and intermediate Naval Flight Officer curriculum in which time-to-train was reduced by 21% for advanced navigation students and 10% for tactical aviation students. "Hands On" flight training was increased

T-2B 153555 from VT-10 with original 2N tail code, in 1974. (Bob Stollof)

12% yet overall squadron flight hours were reduced. The new syllabus was officially introduced on June 6, 1977 with class 7713, comprised of 25 Navy and 5 Marine students. Class 7713 completed the new training program on October 31 1977. This new curriculum was updated and streamlined in June 1979 to better utilize the squadron's assets.

In 1982 VT-10 took delivery of ten T-2B aircraft from storage at MASDC as twelve T-2Cs were transferrd to the basic jet training squadrons. In 1983 five T-2Bs were gained as well as three T-2Cs, and five T-2Cs were transferred out. October 1983 also saw the first T-34Cs arrive to supplement the T-2 in the training role at VT-10. On March 14 1984, the first T-34C Syllabus flight took place and during 1984 twenty T-34Cs were delivered and eight T-2Cs were transferred out. 1985 was started with fifteen T-2Bs and the same aircraft were carried over into 1986.

In the years 1975 through 1986 VT-10 trained many foreign and specialty officers in addition to its Navy and Marine students. These included over 100 Iranian F-14 back seaters, 42 German Rios, 18 Norwegians and 50 Coast Guard navigators. VT-10 also trained 15 Aviation Supply Officers and 23 Aviation Maintenance Duty Officers.

VT-10 has an impressive safety record, with at least twelve Safety Awards, the Captain's Cup six times in a row and the Admiral's Efficiency Award for 1982 and 1984. While flying the T-2 the squadron racked up an impressive record of over 200,000 accident free hours. This record was finally ended on 23 October 1986 when a midair occurred and the pilot of one of the T-2Bs, LT Michael P. Thompson, was killed.

Ex VT-10 T-2B 153542 as seen at the Naval Aviation Museum, NAS Pensacola in 1984. (Bob Stollof)

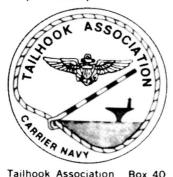

Tailhook Association   Box 40
Bonita, CA 92002

T-2B 155230 of VT-10 in 1984. Rudder is black and white checkerboard and all leading edges are black. Nose numbers and the tail code F are black outlined in white. (USN)

VT-10 T-2C 156712 and T-39D 150980 in a formation turn, note the T-2Cs tailhook is black. (USN, via Tailhook)

T-2C 158898 from VT-10 in 1980, note Safety Award with two hash marks on the nose. (Bob Stolloff)
T-2C 159713 of VT-10 in 1978 with black intake lip and yellow rescue arrow. (USN)

T-2C 158904 from VT-19 in Bicentennial markings of overall white with red and blue trim. The intake warning stripe is red and NAVY and 76 are blue. (Stan Wyckoff)

TRAINING SQUADRON NINETEEN
VT-19

"FROGS"
"ATTACK FROGS"

Training Squadron Nineteen was commissioned on 2 August 1971 at NAS Meridian, Mississippi, as a Basic Jet Training Squadron under the command of CDR. William K. Peery. This commissioning, with the simultaneous establishment of Training Air Wing One, marked the beginning of the single-base training concept with basic and adbanced training under the same Air Wing Commander. Most of the "plankowners" of VT-19 and all of its assets came from its sister squadron, VT-9.

The mission of VT-19 is to conduct basic jet flight instruction in the "Buckeye" jet trainer. The student syllabus consists of jet transition, precision aerobatics, basic and radio instruments, formation, night transition, and air-to-air gunnery. At TAW-1, VT-19 conducts the gunnery training and VT-9 conducts the carrier qualification during the basic jet phase.

To accomplish its mission VT-19 was initially assigned 58 aircraft consisting of 19 T-2As and 39 T-2Bs with 19 of the T-2Bs being configured as gun birds. 31 December 1972 found the squadron with 15 T-2As and 38 T-2Bs. On 20 February 1973 the last T-2A was phased out and VT-19 finished the year with 30 T-2Bs. The T-2Bs were replaced by T-2Cs by May 1974, and 24 T-2Cs were on hand on 31 December 1975.

Squadron strength from 1977 through 1986 was as follows: 19 T-2Cs in 1977, 18 in 1978, 19 in 1979, 19 in 1980, 21 in 1981, 20 in 1982, 21 in 1983, 25 in 1984, 25 in 1985 and 25 in 1986. VT-19 had a secondary mission to train E-2/C-2 pilots from 1983 through 1985. In 1986 VT-7 took over this responsibility and VT-19 was charged with foreign student training.

Training Squadron Nineteen has been consistently commended for its aggressive, all-encompassing safety program, high aircraft availability and training effectiveness. The squadron has received two Meritorious Unit Commendations by the Secretary of the Navy, two Chief of Naval Operations Safety Awards, Two Vice Admiral Goldthwaite Awards and thirteen Chief of Naval Air Training accident free year Awards. The "Frogs" set an all-time record for a jet squadron by completing over 115,000 accident-free hours from commissioning 28 September 1971 to 9 July 1982.

A pre-production Laser Air-to-Air Gunnery System (LATAGS) was installed, starting on 18 October 1985, in four VT-19 T-2Cs for testing in the CNATRA gunnery range. A year's evaluation of the system was planned prior to installation of the production gunsights.

T-2A assigned to VT-19 "Frogs", note black outlines on the white 2M tail codes. (Fred Roos, Naval Fighters)

T-2B 153554 of VT-19 in 1972, note black outline around white 2M. (Fred Roos, Naval Fighters)

2333 Otis, Santa Ana, CA 92704

T-2C 157041 in 1974 with 2M tail code and the green fuselage stripe. (via Burger)

T-2B 152450 of VT-19 on 6-15-74, note two lightning bolts and styleized cat on the nose. (Clay Jansson)

T-2C 159173 of VT-19 with the A tail code, green fuselage stripe and VT-19 insignia on the nose in 1985. (USN)

T-2C 157041 of VT-19 on 5-17-75, note squadron insignia and thin black border around the A tail code. (Swisher)

T-2C 159165 belonging to VT-19 Commanding Officer on 8-30-75, at NAS Moffett Field. (Clay Jansson)

T-2C 158887 of VT-19 banks around the USS Enterprise (CVN-65), off the Coast of San Diego on 9-5-85. (Robert Lawson VT-0495)

T-2C 158604 from VT-23 on 10-20-73 with black and white shark mouth painted on the nose. (Swisher)

THE "PROFESSIONALS" OF

TRAINING SQUADRON TWENTY-THREE VT-23

T-2C 158883 from VT-23 with shark mouth on the nose and City of Minneapolis on the fuselage.

Training Squadron Twenty-Three was originally commissioned as Advanced Training Unit-222 (ATU-222) on 19 November 1958 at NAS Kingsville, Texas. ATU-222 was the first unit in the Naval Air Training Command to employ the supersonic Grumman F11F "Tiger" (TF-11A in 1962). The unit's mission was to provide students with the final phases of advanced jet training prior to their designation as Naval Aviators. Students were taught advanced air-to-air and air-to-ground gunnery, swept-wing jet familiarization, all-weather instrument flight, tactics and formation flight. ATU-222 was redesignated VT-23 in May 1960.

In 1965 the aging TF-11A "Tigers" were replaced by Grumman's TF-9J

"Cougar" with the last "Tiger" student completing the syllabus in June 1965. Also in 1965 rocketry and carrier qualifications were added to the training program.

Five years later, in April 1970, the TF-9Js were replaced by McDonnell-Douglas TA-4J "Skyhawks", with the last "Cougar" being transferred out on 18 September 1970.

In October 1972, under the new "Single Base" concept, VT-23's mission changed to that of a basic jet training squadron. With this mission change came a change to the T-2C "Buckeye". When students complete the basic syllabus at VT-23, they are transferred to VT-21 or VT-22, to receive advanced jet training in the TA-4J "Skyhawk". Upon

successful completion of this training, they are designated Naval Aviators and receive their wings of gold.

VT-23 had a secondary mission to train E-2/C-2 pilots from 1982 through 1985. This mission was handed over to VT-4 in 1985.

The "Professionals" of VT-23 have received numerous awards, including the CNO Safety Award for 1959, 1960, 1981, 1982 and 1983; the CNATRA Safety Award ten times; the Top Jet Squadron for 1967 and 1970; the John H. Tower Trophy in 1970; the VADM Robert Goldthwaite Award for 1973; a Meritorious Unit Commendation for August 1972 through October 1973; and the CNATRA Effectiveness Award for 1984, 1985 and 1986.

T-2C 159166 from VT-23, City of Columbus on 10-13-74. (Clay Jansson)   T-2C 156724 of VT-23 sans shark mouth. (Fred Roos, Naval Fighters)

T-2C 158884 of VT-23 with new B tail code, note City of Waterman written on the fuselage. (Fred Roos, Naval Fighters)

T2-C 158610 with shark mouth and B tail code on 4-12-75. (Swisher)

T-2C 158332 with dark blue tail and nose and red-orange tip tanks, 1976. (Fred Roos, Naval Fighters)

T-2C 158314 from VT-23 on the way to the boat, off NAS Corpus Christi on 7-14-82. (Robert Lawson, Tailhook photo VT-0427)

T-2C 159714 of VT-23 during carrier qualifications   aboard the USS Lexington (AVT-16) on 7-13-82. (Robert Lawson, Tailhook photo VT-0433 and   0431)

T-2C 159170 of VT-23 traps aboard the USS Lexington on 7-13-82. (Robert Lawson, Tailhook VT-0432) T-2C 156686 in 1981 and T-2C 159722 on 8-19-84. Canopy and spine and the stars on the rudder are black, Safety Award with two has marks is red outlined in black. (Smalley)

TRAINING SQUARON TWENTY-SIX VT-26

The "Tigers" of VT-26 were originally commissioned as Advanced Training Unit-223 (ATU-223) at NAS Chase Field. On 1 May 1960, ATU-223 was redesignated VT-23, the squadron was equipped with 45 Grumman F11F-1 (TF-11A in 1962) "Tigers" to fulfill its mission of training students in advanced aerial weapons and tactics. ATU-223 was assigned two other collateral duties: augmenting the Continental Air Defense Force (NORAD) in the interceptor role, and providing familiarization training (FAM) for prospective "Blue Angels".

In 1967 the aging TF-11As were replaced by the Grumman TF-9J "Cougar". The first TF-9J (146378) was received from VT-21 on 2 March and the first F-9 class started on 7 March 1967. The final F-11 student completed flight training on 26 June and the last "Tiger" was transferred out on 13 July 1967.

With the change to the F-9 came a change in the student's syllabus. The Air Defense commitment was deleted and the student training mission was expanded to encompass familiarization, low level navigation, instruments, tactics, air-to-ground weapons delivery, night flying and carrier qualifications.

In 1971, with the advent of the single-base concept, VT-26 was assigned the mission of the basic jet training squadron for Training Air Wing Three. With the change of mission came the T-2C "Buckeye" and a training syllabus consisting of familiarization, instrument flying, night flying, air-to-air gunnery and carrier qualifications. The last F-9 was transferred out on 15 October 1971.

In 1975 VT-26 took on the responsibility for training a Greek Air Force contingent of 28 officers and men. The training was completed on 13 December 1975 and the students went home to fly their T-2E "Buckeyes". In 1976 VT-26 trained an additional three Hellenic pilots. In addition to the Greek pilots VT-26 trained a small number of Venezuelan Air Force pilots who flew the T-2D in Venezuela.

The "Tigers" of VT-26 have received the following awards: Top Advanced Jet Squadron for 1971; the Chief of Naval Operations Safety Award for 1974, 1975, 1977, 1978 and 1983; Meritorious Unit Commendation for 1975; VADM John H. Towers Safety Award for 1975; CNATRA Training Effectiveness Award for 1981 and the CNATRA Safety Award for 1983.

T-2C 159155 of VT-26 on 10-15-74. (Clay Jansson)

T-2C 158324 from VT-26 in overall white with USS Lexington on the fuselage on 10-9-76. (Roy Lock, via Tailhook) T-2C 158888 from VT-26 in standard colors. (USN)

T-2C 158911 of CO of CTW-3, Commodore P.E. "Puff" 'O' Gara. Fuselage stripe is blue with orange comtrawing 3. Rudder stripes are alternating blue, orange, green.

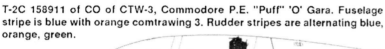

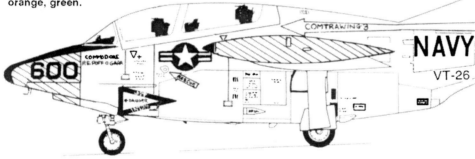

T-2C 159717 of VT-26 and assigned to Commodore P.E. "Puff" 'O' Gara CO of CTW-3 on 10-4-75. Legend on fuselage reads "Irish Men Make Good Pilots, Always In The Air About Something". Shamrock is green. (Clay Jansson)

T-2C 158588 of VT-26 on 4-24-76. (via Smalley)   T-2C 157056 from VT-26 on 10-16-76 in the Spirit of 76 color scheme,   (Clay Jansson)

T-2C 157057 from VT-26 in 1976 in the Spirit of 76 color scheme. see back cover. (Fred Roos, Naval Fighters)

T-2C 156715 from VT-26 practicing FCLP, field carrier landing practice, to prepare for carrier qualifications, at NAS Chase Field on 7-15-82. (Robert Lawson, Tailhook photo VT-0440)

TRAINING SQUADRON   VT-26

A VT-26 T-2C breaks away from T-2C 159723 on 7-15-82, note location of aircraft call number 665 on the lower wing. (Robert Lawson, Tailhook photo VT-0449)

T-2C 157061 from VT-26 preparing to launch from the USS Lexington on 7-13-82. (Robert Lawson, Tailhook photo VT-0446 and 0447)

THE MIRAMAR "BANDITS" FIGHTER SQUADRON VF-126

Commissioned as VA-126 on 6 April 1956, the "Bandits" originally flew Vought F7U-3 Cutlasses. They then transitioned into the F9F-8B "Cougar" and FJ-4B "Fury" and acquired the name "Fighting Sea Hawks". In late 1958 they assumed responsibility for light attack training and flew the A4D Skyhawk in this role as well as the AD-5, 6 and 7 Skyraiders of VA-125 during late 1958 through early 1959. In 1960 VA-126 became the Pacific Fleet instrument Replacement Air Group (RAG) and transitioned to the F9F-8T (TF-9J) "Cougar". In October 1965 VA-126 was redesignated VF-126 and, with the influx of A-4s into the squadron, started providing adversary training through the Viet Nam War years.

Today, the squadron's primary mission is adversary training, with a secondary role of instrument training and a tertiary role of out-of-control (OOC) flight training or spin training. Because VF-126's primary mission changed to adversary training, the squadron's name was changed to "Bandits" in

T-2C 157043 from VF-126 landing at NAS Miramar on 2-16-79. (Robert Lawson, Tailhook photo VT-0332)

T-2C 157053 from VF-126 on a OOC hop on 7-2-80. (Robert Lawson, Tailhook photo VT-0361)

1981.

Increased Combat Air Maneuvering training was resulting in excessive losses of aircraft to out-of-control flight, so, the navy tasked the Navy Test Pilot School with the development of a training program. This program was added to the mission of VF-126 in January 1978 and the T-2C was brought into the squadron to accomplish this mission.

For some time, two spin hops had been used in the Training command to familiarize students to high performance spins in jet aircraft. Since the T-2C had proven its ability to perform and recover positively from upright, inverted and multiple-axis departures and spins without damage to the airframe, it became the logical choice for such training. The training program at VF-126 is viewed as a graduate level program for Pacific Fleet pilots.

T-2B/C STALL AND SPIN CHARACTERISTICS

T-2 DEPARTURE CHARACTERISTICS.
The angle-of-attack system has proven a reliable indicator of departure angle-of-attack, regardless of flap position or gross weight. The departure characteristics of the T-2 aircraft are well defined, preceded by light to mild buffet, and marked by a mild G-break and nose drop caused by airflow separation on the upper surface of the wing. Continued stall penetration results in a mild longitudinal pitching oscillation or porpoise, often accompanied by a wing drop or rolloff to either side. Ailerons remain effctive throughout the stall. Recovery from the departure is immediate when controls are neutralized.

ACCELERATED DEPARTURES.
Accelerated Departures are defined as those entered at load factors greater than 1.0g. Either high or low speed accelerated departures are similar for all aircraft configurations. Actuation of the rudder pedal shaker provides initial warning, and is followed by mild airframe buffet preceding the stall. An accelerated departure is characterized by mild longitudinal pitching oscillations and heavy airframe buffet with little tendency to roll-off. Neutralizing the flight controls will effect immediate recovery.

YAW INDUCED DEPARTURES.
This maneuver is caused by excessive or abrupt rudder application at low to moderate airspeeds and is insidious because of the limited warning of impending departure. At slide/slip angles greater than 15°, the directional stability decreases sharply and is characterized by an abrupt increase in yaw and slight nose rise, followed immediately by an uncontrollable roll in excess of 360°. Neutralizing the controls as the aircraft departs will effect recovery, however the aircraft will possibly roll up to three turns about the longitudinal axis with associated yaw and pitch oscillations before the post stall gyrations stop. Recovery will normally be extremly nose-low or inverted. AOA and airspeed should be checked prior to starting the pull-out to prevent another departure. <u>WARNING</u>: Intentional directional departures are prohibited at airspeeds greater than 160 KIAS to avoid possible overstress.

POST-STALL GYRATION:
If the control inputs are held after the aircraft departs controlled flight, the aircraft will continue to randomly oscillate about any or all axes in increasingly nose-low attitudes which may or may not develop into a spin. From a 1.0g departure, these oscillations are mild with roll in the direction of applied rudder. With ailerons applied opposite to rudder deflection, lower nose-attitudes and faster roll rates will result. Post-stall gyrations resulting from accelerated departures are similar except that intitial roll rates will be higher (assuming the same amount of rudder deflection). In either case, neutralizing the controls will effect rapid recovery, normally in a nose-low upright attitude. AOA and airspeed should be checked prior to starting pull-out.

T-2 SPIN CHARACTERISTICS.
Only intentional erect spins with landing gear, flaps, and speed brakes retracted are allowed in the T-2 aircraft. The aircraft will achieve developed spins to two modes. The non-oscillatory spin mode results when the ailerons and rudder are fully deflected and in opposite directions. The oscillatory spin mode results when the ailerons are fully deflected in the same direction as rudder.

NON-OSCILLATORY SPIN.
The post-stall gyrations for the incipient phase of the non-oscillatory spin entry will require about three turns. Fully deflected pro-spin controls (ailerons and rudder in opposite directions) must be maintained. Characteristics of the steady state spin will include steep nosedown attitudes with some pitching oscillations generally present. Roll rates will vary, with the highest rate associated with the steepest nose-down attitudes. Altitude losses of up to 1500 feet per turn may be expected. Recovery consists of applying full rudder opposite the direction of the turn, and neutralizing elevator and aileron. Initially with the application of recovery controls the roll rate will increase and then rather abruptly stop after approximately two turns. When rotation stops, neutralize the rudder. Recovery will normally be extremely nose low or inverted and AOA and airspeed should be checked prior to starting the pull out.

OSCILLATORY SPINS.
If the spin is entered with the use of aileron and rudder in the same direction, a steady state spin will develop after three or four turns that will be oscillatory in nature. Characteristically, the nose attitude will oscillate from 90° nose-down, to 20° to 30° below the horizon in the incipient phase, with yaw and roll rates slowing when the nose attitude is highest and accelarting in the nose-low attitudes. These oscillations occur approximately once each turn and continue in the steady state spin, with the nose attitudes becoming somewhat lower. If the controls are neutralized just as the nose attitude approaches the highest point and the yaw and roll rates are at their minimum values, the aircraft will normally recover immediately from the post stall gyrations and from the developed spin. However, in all cases positive spin recovery controls (rudder full opposite the turn with elevator and aileron neutral) will effect positive recovery in approximately two turns.

PROGRESSIVE SPIN.
A progressive spin occurs when the aircraft enters a second spin immediately following initial recovery from a developed spin, the direction of rotation normally opposite to that of the original spin. Progressive spins may result from holding in opposite rudder or elevator control forward of neutral after autorotation has stopped, initiating recovery pullout with insufficient airspeed with too much G-force, or some peculiarity of the aircraft. The reversal in rotation will be quite violent, and the spin will tend to be more nose low with faster rotation than the initial spin. Recovery should be initiated immediately, using positive direction of rotation.

FIGHTER SQUADRON VF-43

VF-43 is the East Coast equivalent of VF-126 and is charged with the same missions of adversary training, instrument training, and out-of-control training. The squadron uses the Israli Aircraft Industries "Kfir" (designated F-21A in the U.S.) F-5 "Tigers" and A-4 "Skyhawk" in the adversary role, the TA-4J "Skyhawk" for instrument training and the T-2C "Buckeye" as out-of-control trainers.

T-2C 157041 in 1980. (R. Harrison)

VF-43 was originally established as VF-74A on 1 May 1945 and redesignated VF-74 on 1 August 1945. On 15 November 1946 VF-74 became VF-1B and then VF-21 on 1 September 1948. VF-21 was redesignated VA-43 on 1 July 1959 and flew the A-4 "Skyhawk" as the Atlantic Fleet Instrument Replacement Air Group (RAG). When VA-43's primary mission became adversary training, the squadron was redesignated VF-43 on 1 June 1973.

T-2C 158904 from VF-43 at Nas Oceana on 8-11-82, note Safety Award with two hash marks on the forward fuselage and the VF-43 insignia on the tail. (Robert Lawson, Tailhook photo VT-0464)

T-2C 158904, "TADPOLE" 32 from VF-43 at NAS Oceana in 1986. All markings including the National Insignia are dark gray and the landing gear and gear doors are white.

FS. 35164
INTERMEDIATE BLUE

FS. 36231
DARK GULL GRAY

FS. 36440
GULL GRAY

BLACK

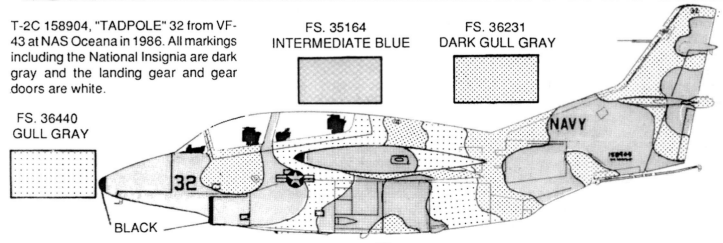

DT-2B 155238 was the last T-2B built, see back cover for colors of this drone director. (Naval Fighters)

DT-2B 155238 on 10-11-75 with medium blue tail stripe and small bat-like insignia above it. (Clay Jansson)

DT-2B 153551 from the Pacific Missile Test Center with the PMTC insignia on the tail over a medium blue stripe. (Mike Grove, Tailhook photo VT-017OV) DT-2C 156721, side number 87 was also operated in this color scheme.

PLASTIC BUCKEYE

The first "Buckeye" in plastic was the airmodel T-2A/B of the early 1970s. This was a 1/72nd scale vacuform kit with fuselages for either the T-2A or the T-2B.

The second kit is the 1/72 Matchbox T-2C kit. Produced in August 1987, the kit contains 32 injection molded pieces in both grey and white plastic. Aside from Matchbox's typically heavy panel lines, the kit does not provide the rear fuselage strakes or tip tank formation lights, but once added, the kit makes up into a excellent model. Markings provided in the kit are for a colorful T-2C of VT-23 or for a Greek Air Force T-2E. If the T-2C is built, the kits yellow orange tip tank and rudder stripes must be replaced with red-orange ones. Thank you matchbox for filling another important gap in Naval Aviation.

NORTH AMERICAN
T·2A/B BUCKEYE

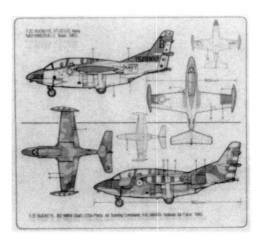

MATCHBOX T-2C/E KIT

2C 159154 of VT-4 in 1986 in special paint scheme to celebrate the 75th anniversary of Naval Aviation. (Bob Stolloff) Colors are white with blue-red-ue rudder, fuselage and tip tank stripes. Upper fin stripes are blue with a red 800 between them. Blue and gold 75th anniversary insignia (as at right) on the tail.

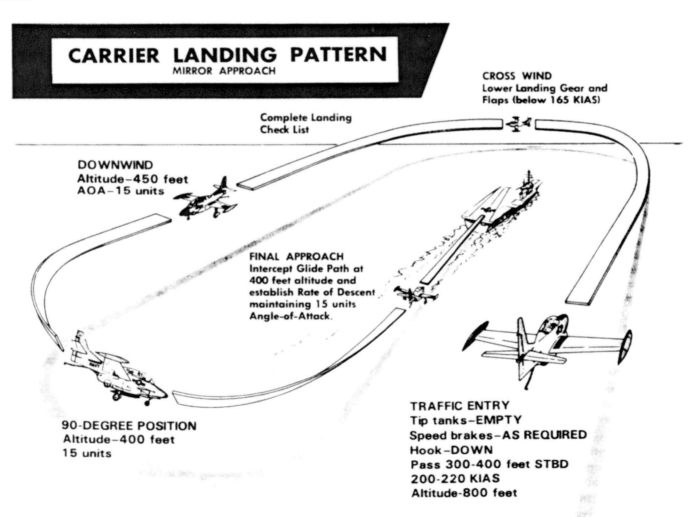

CARRIER LANDING PATTERN
MIRROR APPROACH

CROSS WIND
Lower Landing Gear and
Flaps (below 165 KIAS)

**Complete Landing
Check List**

DOWNWIND
Altitude—450 feet
AOA—15 units

FINAL APPROACH
Intercept Glide Path at
400 feet altitude and
establish Rate of Descent
maintaining 15 units
Angle-of-Attack.

90-DEGREE POSITION
Altitude—400 feet
15 units

TRAFFIC ENTRY
Tip tanks—EMPTY
Speed brakes—AS REQUIRED
Hook—DOWN
Pass 300-400 feet STBD
200-220 KIAS
Altitude—800 feet

CPSIA information can be obtained
at www.ICGtesting.com
Printed in the USA
LVOW09s1211220117
521769LV00015B/1050/P